PRAISE FOR THE
SUCC~~EEDED~~

MW00614959

"Creating innovation and making good things happen in government is not easy. But learning how to do innovation from the founder of a premier innovation unit like AFWERX makes a difficult path clearer. Beam Maue provides a sound guide to creating government innovation, giving us a conceptual framework for approaching the topic, as well as insights from first-hand lessons learned. This unique and insightful book, full of real tools to assist in forming innovation efforts, shows us why AFWERX became such an important innovation effort."

— *Sabra Horne, Chief, CISA Innovation Hub*

(Ms. Horne's professional remarks are her own, and not to be considered representative of the DHS or the US Government)

"We know that organizations benefit greatly from user-friendly processes that bring together data, diversity, and design to inform their choices, and so we were excited to join with AFWERX and share our best practices with one another. Beam's telling - of *The Experiment That Succeeded* will help you see the kind of environment that allows such collaborations to thrive at a world class level."

— *Tom Kehner, Partner, theDifference*

"The men and women who serve in support of our national security deserve access to the best innovation practices and cutting-edge technology that is available. AFWERX is part of a growing network of efforts designed to achieve that outcome, and *The Experiment That Succeeded* offers actionable considerations for building strong, inventive teams that are able to achieve outsized impact."

— MORGAN PLUMMER, NATIONAL SECURITY INNOVATION
NETWORK DIRECTOR

(Mr. Plummer's professional remarks are his own, and not to be considered representative of the DoD or the US Government)

"Innovation and innovation resources are fundamental to our economic prosperity, national defense and security, and day-to-day human flourishing. As a student of how we innovate, I watched from a distance as the United States Department of Defense totally revamped their innovation infrastructure over the past 4-5 years. As I learned when I had Beam as a featured guest on the Next Frontier Podcast: his approach to building AFWERX, his historical and philosophical reference frame, and his keen focus on the human component of innovation processes have given the United States Air Force (and by extension the Department of Defense) an agile, effective, and capable institution of innovation that can adapt with the exponentially changing rate of technology and the increasingly complex geopolitical environment. Beam is a one of a kind innovator, and it has been a pleasure following his work."

— MAX GOLDBERG, INVESTOR, FUTURIST, NEXT FRONTIER PODCAST HOST

"Our nation needs catalysts who can create game-changing solutions to troubling challenges by capitalizing upon the skills of the private sector and the armed forces. *The Experiment That Succeeded* provides an understanding of how to be a catalyst as Beam provides principles and structures that can also be put into successful practice. This is a useful read whether you are on the government or private sector part of an innovation team."

— BRIAN LIESVELD, EXECUTIVE DIRECTOR, DEFENSEWERX

"Startup companies who are trying to offer their capabilities for government use often encounter a tangled web of confusing bureaucracy that frustrates and deters businesses from ever wanting to work with the government again. AFWERX and the US Air Force have been experimenting with new, simpler, business-friendly approaches, and *The Experiment That Succeeded* gives you engaging insight into the mindsets and actions that made that possible, from the insider's perspective of their startup years leader Beam."

— *ANDREW BAIR, PARTNER, SWAY VENTURES*

"Beam is a clear voice in a sea of noise. This book shows how we can make innovation happen within government and private companies alike. Engaging and substantive."

— *SVEN WEIZENEGGER CEO, CYBER INNOVATION HUB*

THE EXPERIMENT THAT SUCCEEDED

HOW A GOVERNMENT STARTUP BEAT
AMAZON, LEVERAGED INNOVATION HISTORY
AND CHANGED AIR FORCE CULTURE

BRIAN E.A. "BEAM" MAUE, PHD

Dedicated with gratitude
to those Spirits who are driven
to experiment and advance innovations...
...our future will be shaped by their deeds.

CONTENTS

INTRODUCTION

This book explores one simple but ever-troubling question:

Why do some government innovation efforts succeed while others fizzle and fade?

There are many answers to that question, and these pages examine how the evidence reveals a set of common factors key to achieving innovation success. My own experiences grappling with these factors were strongest when I was leading the AFWERX (pronounced "aff-works") innovation organization during our startup years. It is my hope that these insights will prove useful to you and your own innovation efforts.

AFWERX was created in the midst of urgency and uncertainty. In the summer of 2017, the senior leaders of the US Air Force issued a document declaring the Air Force's most important strategic priorities. Priority #3 was "Drive innovation...to secure our future." This led to a Pentagon effort to solicit ideas, frameworks and leaders for a new innovation mission; the name "AFWERX" did not even yet exist. I volunteered to contribute my vision and approach, and was selected to be part of the initial steering committee for AFWERX's formation. In early 2018, I was asked to become the AFWERX Mission Lead and transition AFWERX from a committee-style method of guidance to a single, unified vision for operations. I discussed that request, and its significant time impact, with my wife Karin. With her support, I accepted the duty.

In the summer of 2020, as AFWERX was concluding our third year in existence, we were ranked *16th in the world* as a Best Workplace for Innovators by Fast Company's annual innovation evaluation process. They had analyzed 865 organizations from around the globe, and our ranking placed us ahead of other world-class innovators such as Amazon and Intel.

I was pleasantly surprised to see that our talented people were recognized for their incredible efforts. At the same time, it was never our goal to win world-class recognition. Earning that world-class accolade was a welcomed by-product of our continuous learning and experimentation, but the core AFWERX mission was always to help solve our warfighters' challenges—and we did not do that alone.

Critical portions of our best innovation practices came from our business partners such as theDifference, ROCeteer and Capital Factory as well as our nonprofit partners such as Virginia Tech-Applied Research Cooperation (VT-ARC), DEFENSEWERX and the National Security Innovation Network (NSIN). With their collaboration (and in under three years), AFWERX went from an idea written by one person to a small core team who, with the help of a motivated *Coalition of the Willing,* collectively produced innovations such as:

- Connecting over 60,000 military, academic and business members (a majority of the business members had never worked with the government previously)
- Attracting **over $1 billion** in private capital for Air

Force technology development interests, saving
taxpayers significant development costs
- Creating volunteer (and productive!) innovation
  teams and offices at over 70 Air Force bases
- Helping solve over 250 challenges through
  prototyping and technology evaluations
- Forging a COVID-19 response process that was
  leveraged by the federal government

AFWERX did not come ready-made with obvious plans
and processes, and so we had to learn and experiment our way
through numerous difficulties and obstacles. There was no
obvious blueprint for connecting government, business, and
academic capabilities in a manner that would create greater
agility for our 680,000-member organization as well as our
nation's defense. Creating and growing AFWERX was like
solving a challenging puzzle where all the pieces were the
same color and the puzzle's final shape was not known in
advance.

It took time to assemble and create a relevant set of best
practices from organizations and organizational research. We
looked for successful factors from across history, spanning from
Sun Tzu to Silicon Valley. Much of that learning was integrated
"on the fly" as we were growing, or as we often said back then:
"We are building the AFWERX plane while it is already in
flight." Such was the pace of fast development and results
during our startup years of 2017 to 2020.

Our mission had an extra challenge as well. We had to
assemble our innovation system within the bulky and
constrained government bureaucracy of the Department of
Defense (DoD). The DoD's structure had emerged over time
from good intentions to responsibly handle taxpayer dollars,
but what "responsibly handle" often meant consisted of thousands upon thousands of pages of rules, policies and laws that

hindered agile contracting actions, limited marketing efforts and slowed personnel hiring.

While useful and well-intentioned, many of those historical rules simply were not current enough to allow innovation to flow freely. Of course, this type of bureaucracy is not unique to the DoD. It exists at the federal, state and city levels, as well as any government institution where taxpayer dollars are involved.

Whatever degree of government bureaucracy that you are facing, this book examines the major frameworks, mindsets and considerations that helped AFWERX achieve its ranking and its many accomplishments...even within a government setting. Hopefully, by learning from our experiences and seeing our journey unfold ahead of (or in tandem with) your own, you will not have to take the same wild ride that we did on the learning curve. Our AFWERX journey does not offer any single answer to the innovation question. However, it does offer considerations (and a few warnings) about how to build and advance your innovation mission within the government—no matter how daunting that mission may seem some days.

Now, let us begin to connect some dots...

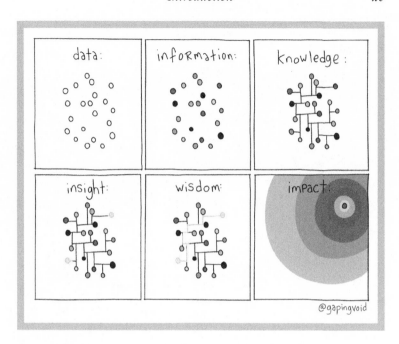

CREATING INNOVATION FLOW

AN ALL-TOO-COMMON GOVERNMENT BLOCKAGE

There is a minimal—and some might say "negative"—incentive structure within government when it comes to innovation. Consider this chain with four links:

1. Our bulky government bureaucratic system prefers (understandably) to promote people who do not fail. Somebody with a reputation for failing is less likely to be promoted.

2. Maintaining the status quo is a way for many government workers to "not fail."

3. Yet innovation requires experiments, and many people's experiments do "fail." For example, Thomas Edison failed with over 3,000 thoughts and experiments during his quest to invent a useful lightbulb.

4. Therefore, government members who start or join an innovation effort risk missing career promotions due to the "failures" —or at least the risks of unsuccessful results—that can occur within their innovation experiments.

Together, these linked conditions shackle the mindsets of many government members and make them less inclined to try innovating. To help you and others find ways to break through these and other government limitations, we are going to journey together through a framework that describes the *Factors Linking Organizational Will* for innovation efforts; it is the framework that I developed within AFWERX for focusing on all of the efforts that would be necessary for our success. It is a mouthful of a description, so I abbreviated it as the *FLOW* model. As the full name suggests, the model focuses on our *will*. Why? Read on, brave innovators...

WILL IS AT THE HEART OF ANY EFFORT

Committing our energy to an effort that has a chance of "failing" requires courage. Courage is the *will* to take action when there are known risks, and it is distinct from a foolhardy "we can do anything" attitude. Careless innovators filled with ignorant bravado are more inclined to take unnecessary risks, and adding more risks to an already risky mission increases the chances of failure. Remember, failure is not something that the government's many "judges"—such as government supervisors, contracting officers and lawyers—want to support, and their aversion to risk is understandable.

Even so, not all risk is the same. Some risk is manageable— otherwise, why would we get up every day, sit in vehicles that weigh thousands of pounds and accelerate to death-producing speeds while performing the uncoordinated dance of daily driving with hundreds of strangers? We "risk" driving every day because there are already a number of factors for successful driving in place, including commonly understood rules that allow for independent actions so that people can reach their desired destinations. As this example hopefully illustrates, courage and intelligence about an *Environment's* risk can guide us to understand what influences acceptable risk levels.

Whether you are driving a car or driving innovation, it is easier to generate the *will* to take action when there is a flexible structure of guidance within which to operate. For example, the 2018 National Defense Strategy included the guidance to "shed outdated management practices and structures while integrating insights from business innovation." Those stated priorities helped generate support from our senior leaders, as well as our AFWERX partners and allies, to create processes that would allow our innovation efforts to flow more freely. Leadership support can appear in many forms, including the often-overlooked form of a policy change. Policies that increase flexibility can motivate you through the darker times, when progress is not occurring as quickly as desired.

Understanding the common factors that influence how to generate *will* can greatly aid our causes, whether they are for innovation efforts or other goal-oriented objectives. Alternatively, a lack of situational awareness of these elements can kill an effort early. The *FLOW* model encourages multi-layer, multi-stakeholder perception. We will examine each layer in more detail in the coming chapters, so for the moment, a glimpse of the full model is:

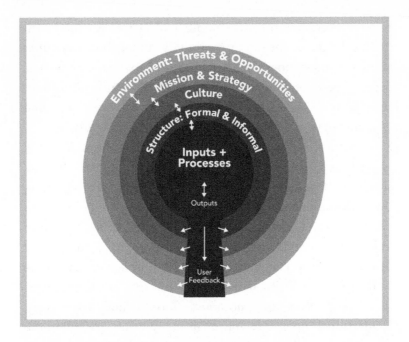

As you journey through the *FLOW* model, you will begin to see how each layer supports or hinders the others while working through key innovation tasks such as:

- Starting or expanding your program
- Producing prototypes
- Explaining the program to people who control resources that you could use
- Building an inspiring culture
- Holding a strategy meeting (and holding meetings in general)
- Communicating success and "failure" (hint: within an <u>experimental</u> culture of innovation, it is only "failure" if nothing is learned)

The *FLOW* model, like any model, deliberately presents an incomplete abstraction of the world. Much like a map, it is the model's simplifications that provide its usefulness. The *FLOW* model provides insights into personal and organizational *will* much like Abraham Maslow's Hierarchy of Needs provides insights into human behavior. Whether you are performing innovation efforts for the Air Force's 680,000 members or creating a new project with a team of six or eight members, this model will help focus your scanning of a situation as well as your thoughts and your energy. The *FLOW* model was created in the spirit of George Box's observation that "All models are wrong, but some are useful." *FLOW's* simplifications can provide quick insights that solve situations, particularly when dealing with abstract concepts such as the *will* and "probabilities of success."

THOUGHT EXPERIMENT: PROBABILITIES OF TRUE SUCCESS

Probabilities and statistics can be deceiving. It is a sentiment captured by at least one humorous expression: "There are three kinds of lies: lies, damned lies and statistics." Often, the "lie" is that some statistical number is being used to claim that some *factor X* caused *outcome Y*. As a thought experiment on how easily that misinterpretation of causal relationships can happen, please imagine 64 people standing in a large room, each with a quarter in their hand. One person on the sidelines shouts "Flip!" and all 64 people toss up their coins, catch them and look to see if the side showing is heads or tails.

"Those of you with tails may exit," declares the announcer, and half of the people depart the room. The coin-flipping experiment is repeated with the remaining 32 people and this time 16 tails are flipped, so 16 people exit the room. After another flip, eight leave. Then four. Then two. Finally, one person flips tails and exits, leaving just one person in the room who has flipped heads six times in a row.

Because you know that there were 64 people at the start of the experiment, and that the odds were that 50 percent of participants would see heads after a flip (assuming a fairly weighted quarter), you are probably not surprised to see one person left in the room who flipped heads six times in a row. It is also possible that two or three people could still be standing there, or that zero people could be left. Even so, the highest odds suggest that somebody should have flipped six heads in a row without possessing any particularly unique skill for coin-flipping.

As a contrast, imagine that you walked into the room at the end of the flip-and-exit routine, but you did not know 64 people had been involved in a coin-flipping experiment moments earlier. Instead, you just happened to casually walk into a room where a person just flipped heads six times in a row. Suppose that the lone flipper turns to you and says, "Heads up! I just flipped a head six times in a row, when the odds against that are something like 98.5 percent. Would you like to hire me to flip coins for you?" Intrigued, you turn to the only other person in the room (the announcer) and ask if the flipper's claim is true. The person concurs.

Without the prior knowledge that there were 64 people in the room at the start of this experiment, you might be impressed at the results and the "skill" the coin-flipper claims to have—even the coin flipper might sincerely believe that she has a unique skill! However, we know that the flipper just happened to be the statistically lucky one within a random trial of 64 people. The flipper did not "cause" the six heads to occur. Random chance was involved. It is highly unlikely that her six heads will be repeated in her next flipping attempts.

Successful innovation is much harder than a random 50/50 chance or even a series of 50/50 chances. There is no guarantee that even one innovation effort will be successful, even if you start with 100 distinct efforts or projects. At the same time, the first three years of AFWERX demonstrated that using certain principles, guided by the *FLOW* model, can help "cause" hundreds, and then thousands, of successful innovations across the Air Force, the DoD and the United States government more generally.

Any evaluation of our startup years must include an acknowledgement that AFWERX definitely experienced "luck" a time or two (or more). In general, however, we were very deliberate in our choices and did not use a random, unin-formed mindset of "Let's just try A, and if that doesn't work, we'll try approach B." We of AFWERX were more inclined to exemplify Louis Pasteur's (inventor of vaccines and more) observation that:

Chance favors only the prepared mind.

The *FLOW* model's considerations and the explorations

that follow can help guide innovation efforts to better results. Each of the following factor chapters will conclude with questions that will allow you to analyze how to account for non-random components you can influence. As we journey into the *FLOW* factors, as well as innovative considerations from AFWERX and non-AFWERX insights, we will see how the success of AFWERX's first three years was not random—the linking of success factors is repeatable.

JUGGLING CHAINSAWS WHILE TIGHTROPE WALKING THROUGH A STORM

The previous eight-word heading was the original title for this book. I started drafting this book long before we were awarded our world-class ranking, and that first title was designed to warn readers that building the capacity for world-class innovation in the government is not a dreamy experience filled with gumdrops, lollipops and unicorns. The *will* of

AFWERX was tested on multiple occasions during our startup years. At times, it seemed as though not quite everyone had received the memo from the Air Force and DoD leaders to "drive innovation." The tightrope walker picture above symbolizes to me just how challenging government innovation can be. To elaborate, trying to innovate in government is like:

Juggling: You will need to juggle multiple priorities at any time, such as people, relationships, tech projects, thought leadership and *FLOW* assessments.

Chainsaws: There are many ways to handle priorities, and many approaches can create painful outcomes—but there are also safe ways to handle them.

Tightrope: Even as you handle your priorities, you will be expected to remain within a narrow band of approved, regulated behavior.

Walking: Forward progress will be expected; without positive results, senior leadership support, support from others and resourcing may fade.

Through: Although innovating in government may be incredibly challenging, it can become less stormy and more stable with success.

Storm: There will be elements all around you that will make your efforts more difficult. It is not personal; just the nature of bureaucracy and its risk-averse judges, such as supervisors and lawyers.

Rainbow: Your fulfilling efforts will lead to a brighter future.

Smiling: A fulfilling life experience includes purpose, challenge and growth. Innovative efforts, and creative efforts more generally, offer fulfillment.

Clouds: There will always be clouds. There is no perfect, clear vision of the future.

Now that we have looked at the big picture overview of our journey, it is time to go with the *FLOW* and begin analyzing innovation success factors in greater detail. Be warned: as we expand our experimental mindset and situational awareness, we will develop more ways to rearrange reality. The simultaneous effects may impact our ways of thinking so much so that we may observe a phrase such as "Elvis lives" and then instantly think "Hey, those two words have the same letters used differently twice in a row!" An innovative mind likes to play and see the world with different views.

Welcome! Let the juggling commence!

2

ENVIRONMENT:

THE FIRST REASON

Once upon a time, three people used three separate doors to enter a spacious and completely dark room. They were told that the first person to correctly guess the object in the center of the room would receive $500, and so they started inching toward the center of the blackness with their arms extended, scanning the space in front of them. As their bodies moved about, suddenly one person shouted out, "Found it! It's a rope!"

"Incorrect," an authoritative voice said from within the room.

A second person exclaimed, "Hah! No, I can feel it now...it's a tree trunk."

"Incorrect."

When the third person spoke, she was calmer than the others. "You both missed the spiked spear I have encountered over here. So...if there is also a rope and big rounded log of wood, then this must be some kind of giant crossbow."

"Incorrect," said the voice.

The lights were turned on, and as the people's eyes adjusted to the brightness, the object that came into focus was a well-trained circus elephant, standing incredibly still with its tail, legs and tusks nearly motionless.

This elephant tale highlights the problems that can arise from limited impressions. How easily can a misunderstanding of an *Environment* take us to an incorrect analysis? Even when combined with prior information and other people's measurements, our partial views of the world are no guarantee that we will have a clear understanding of the present. The elephant-in-the-room question about the future is even more daunting: if the present is this difficult to understand, how much less can we see and understand about the future?

For example, in the mid-1980s, could anyone have predicted the way world maps would have to be redrawn by the dawn of the new millennium? The Berlin Wall fell, the Soviet Union dissolved and Yugoslavia broke into segments. After the year 2000 arrived, more concepts about the *Environment* were upended. The concept of a "national power" became less certain when America suffered her greatest loss of life from an attack on American soil—and unlike the attack on Pearl Harbor on December 7, 1941, that September 11, 2001 attack was not even from another "nation." The very definition of the word "attack" became even blurrier in 2014 when a foreign entity used cyber capabilities to attack Sony Pictures Entertainment. No bombs were dropped, yet damage was accomplished.

The 2014 cyberattack was another in a series of evolutions (and at times, revolutions) in computing and artificial intelligence (AI) capabilities. In the 1980s, the idea of a computer beating a human in chess was laughable, but in 1997, IBM's Deep Blue computer program defeated world chess champion Gary Kasparov. It was a major milestone in the advance of computing intelligence, but many opinionated voices at the time claimed it was only a minor event because chess was computationally "simple." With only 64 squares, it was argued, a chess board was rather constrained when factoring in the rules-based moves of its pieces. Chess only offered about 20 to 40 options per turn, and thus it was inevitable that computers would eventually have enough memory and calculating power to predict all future moves, choose the best percentage move for a given turn and overtake any human's best prediction of five or six moves ahead. In other words, the entire chess *Environment* could be known and conquered by a computer opponent.

Skeptics believed that a more challenging *Environment* for AI would be the ancient game of Go. Go is possibly the oldest board game ever played. With its board grid of 19 x 19 interlocking lines, it often offers more than 200 options per turn. Computers would not be able to predict all of the billions of remaining moves within a game, and so Go could not be conquered by a machine. A different kind of intelligence besides "know everything" would be needed—and it was created! Although it took another two decades after Deep Blue's victories, Deep Mind's AlphaGo computer program defeated Go world champion Lee Sedol in 2016. The AI was not based on knowing everything that would occur; instead, its learning and training approach was based on limited probabilities within regions of selected importance on the Go board. A different approach to intelligence had been needed to solve a more complex problem, and innovative minds found a way to create it for an *Environment* where everything could not always be known.

This AI evolution highlights a key question:

"What is intelligence?"

You can spend hours in a college classroom trying to pin down an answer to this question—and I actually did when I was teaching at the United States Air Force Academy. It was a great exercise to listen to young cadets provide examples of intelligence.

For the first part of a class, they usually shared stories about intelligence that had been demonstrated by other cadets. They were asked, "How do you know someone is intelligent?" And they responded with evidence such as:

"They get good grades."

"They make the right moves during sports competitions."

"They always provide great dinner-and-a-movie suggestions."

Eventually, the class of cadets would converge upon a phrase that would be abstract enough to cover these kinds of examples, yet specific enough that they could start targeting how to become more intelligent. The answer? There are many, but the one that I prefer is:

"Intelligence is the ability to accurately predict."

History has shown that one of the key differences between successful and unsuccessful people is their ability to predict how a set of actions—or adjustments to their planned actions—will make them more likely to achieve an anticipated outcome. Athletes, coaches and military members who antici-pate their opponents' moves are more likely to achieve victo-ries. Business people who anticipate their customers' needs earn greater sales, market share and company success. Across all fields of life, greater prosperity is associated with those who have the *intelligent* ability to "see" which actions have the highest probability of leading to the right results. With regard to *successful* innovation efforts, we can distinguish between those who pursue innovation and those who pursue *intelligent* innovation.

Did you notice that our definition of intelligence included the word "predict" but not "guarantee?" Life is complex, and there are a number of factors external to your innovation efforts that can affect your success or failure. For example, consider how intelligent, entrepreneurial people who opened their first restaurant or gym in the spring of 2020 would have been negatively impacted by the COVID-19 virus. The entrepre-neurs may have had a great plan and tremendous *will*, but their efforts were diminished or negated by a bad external *Envi-ronment*.

Indeed, "*Environment* happens" is a G-rated version of a more profane phrase that speaks to negative events that occur outside of our control. On a day-to-day basis, if our *Environment* always remained the same, it would be of little interest to us once we mastered it. However, as even our brief examples have demonstrated, our *Environment* is in a state of constant change. These conditions of change create two categories within the outer rung of our *FLOW* model:

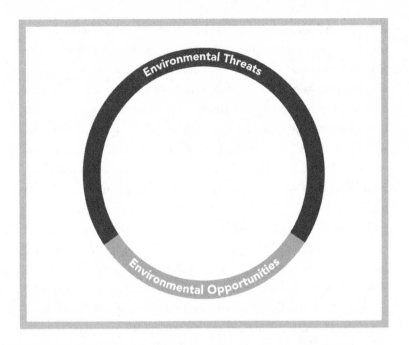

CATEGORY 1: CHANGE AS A THREAT

One of the first utterances of the now clichéd phrase "the only constant thing is change" was from the ancient Greek philosopher Heraclitus, who advised that "You cannot step into the same river twice." Of course, he was right: evolutions and revolutions continually occur, and there is no such thing as an *Environment* that stands still. Written differently, if the rest of the participants in an *Environment* are racing to advance their position while you and your organization are staying the same, then you are falling behind.

Even so, an organization cannot ever truly stay the same—even if its members are intentionally trying to maintain their status quo. Such attempts will lose out to atrophy and entropy. These two concepts may be bluntly bundled together into one simple warning:

"All things lose energy and break down over time."

When we stop exercising, our muscles weaken. When we stop changing the oil in our cars, the cars quit working. Atrophy and entropy always occur. No "thing" on Earth, including ourselves, can ever stay the same. It follows, then, that we must always analyze, refresh and grow our capabilities —such as through *FLOW* scanning of our circumstances—lest our *will* diminish. Staying static is an actual impossibility. For these reasons, we may label "Change within our *Environment*" as a threat.

Non-action on the part of a government organization (or any organization) will lead to its degradation, and possibly its future irrelevance and elimination. The bankruptcy of the Kodak film company demonstrates the peril of not adapting to change. Even though Kodak invented one of the first digital cameras, Kodak clung to its film-based history and was slow to embrace the changing preference of customers for digital photography. *Environment* happened, and Kodak went bankrupt. We should scan and shape our *Environment*, or we end up reacting to it with less *will*, or even no *will*, as our organization ceases to exist.

The difference between the US government and a private sector company such as Kodak is that the government can, unfortunately, "afford" to be slow to change, be unprofitable and still exist. In fact, the government is incredibly unprofitable and indebted. Our US debt is an incomprehensible $23 trillion at the time of this book's writing. This equates to approximately $70,000 of national debt per US citizen. The majority of citizens have not ever saved $70,000, and a majority of households earn less than $70,000 during an entire year! Even though the debt represents millions of life years of labor from our citizens, because of the government's size and status in the global *Environment*, it can accept more *will*-degrading debt. Until it cannot.

At that point, it will be too late. Without a felt, imminent threat of collapse, our leaders are likely to continue avoiding making hard financial decisions and will continue allowing the government to perform poorly with an unbalanced budget that will eventually cripple us. American leaders lack the incentives to make our government profitable or even balance the budget. Voters can help change that, but they are also busy with their lives and cannot babysit the elected leaders during each law-making and funding decision. We do not have to wait for those leaders to become responsible. With innovation, we can create ways to perform more effectively and more efficiently.

Until now, we have avoided defining "innovation" within this book because we needed to glimpse at a number of concepts first, such as intelligence, probabilities, *Environment* and the *will*. We have now arrived at a place where we can offer a definition of "innovation" that will serve as a foundation for the rest of this book. More specifically:

Innovation is the act of creating an alternate reality.

When we innovate, we create alternate realities. Sometimes an innovation is a highly probable result of hypothesis testing and sometimes an innovation is a happy accident. Sometimes an innovation is a new widget and sometimes it is a new thought that changes conversations, mindsets and policies. Whether an idea advances as a doodle on the back of a napkin or because a prototype produces new data, the innovation process advances our thoughts, actions and future options in ways never before known. Each innovative effort reveals new insights to follow or warnings about what *not* to follow.

NEW WAYS OF SEEING THE WORLD REQUIRE NEW EYES TO SEE THEM WITH

@gapingvoid

CATEGORY 2: CHANGE AS AN OPPORTUNITY

A tale from ancient China tells of two village farmers who often met to discuss current events every morning at a wooden fence that divided their properties. One Monday morning, the farmer from the first farm said, "Those sure were some howling winds during last night's storm, eh?"

"Indeed," said the second farmer.

"Well, it looks like a section of your horse's corral in the back was blown down and that your horse has run away. Such a bad turn of events."

"Hmmm...maybe bad, maybe good...we will see," said the second farmer. After the two parted, the second farmer repaired his broken corral.

The next morning, the two met at the fence, and the first neighbor said excitedly, "You have three horses grazing in your front lawn! Your horse must have attracted two wild horses to come back with him! Such good luck..."

"Hmmm...maybe good, maybe bad," said the second farmer. After the two parted, the second farmer went and guided the horses to the inside of the recently repaired corral.

On Wednesday morning, the two neighbors met again, and the first neighbor said, "Finally, a day without any drama at your house."

"Not really," said the second farmer, "My son tried to tame the wild horses yesterday. The first horse went pretty easy, but the second horse bucked my son off and broke my boy's leg."

"Oh, such bad luck," said the first neighbor.

"Hmmm...maybe bad, maybe good," said the second farmer, and he went off to tend to his son.

On Thursday, military leaders came through the village to draft an army. When they saw that the second farmer's son had a broken leg, they did not take him.

When the first neighbor heard about this, he exclaimed to the second farmer, "Such good fortune!"

"Maybe..."

According to US budget data, the government has not kept pace with the alternate reality creation efforts of private sector companies. For example, the Congressional Budget Office has estimated that the private sector collectively became the leader for research and development (R&D) efforts in the United States starting around 1980. Since then, the gap between industry and government research has grown to a ratio of nearly 3:1 in favor of industry, as industry spent $333 billion on R&D while the government spent $116 billion (based on data from 2015).

Should we panic? Was this change a sign of our government's imminent collapse? Maybe, or maybe not. This insight from the Congressional Budget Office also suggests that our government—and our innovation efforts in government—

could be more effective if we integrated some of the policies, processes and solutions available from industry. We are fortunate to have an *Environment* where change is being championed by our own nation's established businesses and entrepreneurial community. Our AFWERX innovation effort relied heavily upon this opportunity in our *Environment* during our startup years. We partnered with businesses such as ROCeteer Inc, theDifference, and Capital Factory, as well as nonprofits such as VT-ARC, NSIN and DEFENSEWERX, to add skill sets to our mission capabilities.

We could not afford to be sluggish. There are some nations that have been advancing their R&D efforts at rates that are competitive with—and at times leading—the US. For example, there are unclassified news stories of other nations advancing the development of hypersonic nuclear weapons, artificial intelligence and quantum computing capabilities. Much like our national debt, the full threat of these changes has not been felt by our leaders. Although some leaders have been slow to counter emerging threats as well as offer debt reduction opportunities, we can use innovation to reduce these threats if we can generate the *will* to do so.

Have you ever seen one of those Rorschach inkblot tests? This psychological tool of ink images offers counselors a possible way for understanding their patients' perspectives. For example, imagine that you are a psychologist who separately meets five new patients in one day. As part of your initial gatherings, you show each of them a series of inkblot images. Imagine that they each responded to the first inkblot picture that they see in the following way:

Patient #1: "It looks like a butterfly!"
Patient #2: "Butterfly."
Patient #3: "Awww, it's a butterfly!"
Patient #4: "A bully swinging his fists and kicking his legs at me."
Patient #5: "A blurry butterfly in flight."

What might you conclude? Perhaps you might suspect that

Patient #4 has been influenced by a bully from an earlier experience in life. When people respond to the same experience differently, you have a chance to learn a little bit more about them. If you are able to be aware of your responses even as you observe others' reactions, then you also have opportunities to learn about how you perceive your *Environment* as compared to others.

With regard to government innovation, leaders must take the time to discern how their *Environment* has two different types of inkblot readers. Innovation and experiments are by their very nature a bit non-linear. Innovation cannot be a precise, step-by-step calendar of events that guarantees a successful outcome on a precise date. Unfortunately, many of the current government regulations do not account for that.

@gapingvoid

TWO INKBLOT READING MINDSETS

During AFWERX's startup years, we encountered two different types of inkblot readers. One group in our shared *Environment* of US government wanted to know <u>precisely</u> what taxpayer money was buying and why that was allowed. Their minds were guided by a simple thought: "If I cannot find a written reference that says this action or thing may be attempted by a government member, then I shall not approve it." This "precise, positive wording must be found" group of people became very nervous when they were asked to review a proposal of "try something new." Their guiding regulations, written in the past, typically did not contain language specifically written for what we were seeking to do—our efforts were too new. Sometimes we would even be told, "We are rewriting the regulation, but for now, these are the rules." Does that even make sense?! The approving authorities knew that a regulation needed to be updated, and it was in the process of being changed, but they would not want to write a waiver letter to let us proceed. Their actions challenged our *will*.

In their hearts, these review judges were only trying to do their jobs, which largely appeared to revolve around their interpretation of keeping their government organization out of trouble. As a result, they were likely to resist "try something new" proposals because those did not fit within the judges' narrow perceptions of what they were supposed to do. They were not mean people. They were simply risk-averse bureaucrats. They would offer advice ("No") and needed someone else to be accountable for the decision. Sometimes we could reach a senior leader who would override the review judges, but not always.

The second group of project inkblot readers that we encountered viewed new innovation efforts from a lens of "If it is not declared illegal and I can confidently tell my grandma or children what I am doing with a clean conscience, then I will authorize the innovators to try it." It was a simple morality and integrity test for taxpayer dollar usage. These "unless it is illegal" people lived with a much greater openness for "try something new." They had their standards for morality and integrity, but they could also see the bigger picture. For example, some could point to the United States' early "startup" years and see the flexible, innovative wisdom of our Founding Fathers in statements such as the Tenth Amendment to the Constitution:

The powers not delegated to the United States by the Constitution,
nor prohibited by it to the states, are reserved to the states
respectively, or to the people.

The Founding Fathers were well aware of the need to avoid rigid constraints within our young country. They did not believe that everything needed to be written down in order for it to be legal. Instead, if it was not written down as illegal, it might be open for trying.

The Founders also established our nation with flexibility and tolerance for disagreement. Indeed, America's greatness was not built upon 100 percent agreement and approval consensus. Instead, America's leadership and governance advanced on the basis of a majority vote. "Fifty percent plus one" has not been a perfect system, and it can become a bit tricky to explain at times when it comes to the Electoral College. However, the democratic approach of the United States has proven to be world-impacting.

Consensus-based, 100 percent agreement and approval reviews of projects are not democratic reviews. Within a consensus approach, just one person or agency can disagree about a project's approach and everything grinds to a halt. One nervous lawyer, one uninformed supervisor or one "I'm too busy to study this and hear your appeal right now" member of a project review team can freeze an innovation effort, and then atrophy and entropy take their toll on an innovation team's *will*.

Achieving consensus at every step of an innovation effort comes at a cost of time. If you are subjected to a consensus-based project review group within your *Environment*, then one effective approach (although it is not time-efficient) is to over-communicate to all of the project's members in advance of any meetings so that decisions can be made at the meetings. This costs you extra time to prepare "read ahead" packages of papers and slides, and at times it can feel like you are doing other people's jobs and thinking for them. (If you really do have a good idea, sometimes the additional group review of the idea can sharpen it—not always, but sometimes.)

There is no easy rule for a question such as "How many reviews are enough?" Perhaps an answer of "As few as possible to feel 80 percent comfortable with proceeding" would apply to an innovation effort. During our startup years, AFWERX bene-fited from Lt Gen J.D. Harris, the Air Force's deputy chief of staff for plans and programs. He gave me the guidance:

"Beam, if AFWERX is not failing at least 70 percent of the time, then I am going to wonder if you are really trying to innovate."

Having access to a supportive senior leader can greatly enhance an innovation team's *will*.

Innovation projects offer fascinating inkblots by which to learn more about reviewers' mindsets. If reviewers look at a project for flaws, then they will find flaws; finding flaws is easy. If reviewers want to be safer, they will always find ways to be safer and burn down risk with additional reviews and analysis. Unfortunately, this leads to "paralysis by analysis."

It may go without saying, but innovation can be choked by review team members with zero-risk mindsets, and "safer" needs to be measured against actual harm from non-success. If an innovation effort fails and it has followed the "start small" approach we will speak about in the upcoming *Mission and Strategy* factors, then any harm from a non-success will almost always be minimal (assuming that the non-success is a techno-logical one, not a relationship one).

If you work within a consensus *Environment*, then early participation and engagement from all of an *Environment's* stakeholders is important in order for a project to be successful. During our early days, AFWERX endured a number of reviews from people whose opinion was based on the thought: "This was not my idea, and I would not have done it like this, so it is too risky for me to approve it." However, when these judges were approached while we were still refining an idea, the judge would be more inclined to approve the idea that they had helped shape. When you are a "try something new" program in the government, even if you have senior leader support, a lot of bureaucratic mid-level people can make your mission very difficult. We did not get to control that part of the innovation process, and so communicating early and often to all of a project's stakeholders became a notable consideration within our government consensus *Environment*.

By contrast, many startup firms in the private sector are able to start with a relatively clean slate. They may hire who they want, and quickly. Private sector firms can also take more risks, whether based on democratic majority voting or even by one leader simply saying "make it so." Whether they are a few people working out of a garage or a slightly larger team with venture capital backing, private sector startup companies can often quickly reach a project decision and keep progressing forward. They can also increase the size of their efforts as profits roll in, whereas government innovation efforts may have to wait for annual budget reviews before acquiring more fund-ing. These contrasts could sometimes dampen our *will*, but we also reminded ourselves that there are some advantages to innovating within government, such as a very low risk of going bankrupt (versus private industry's pressure to quickly make profits or perish).

Fortunately, after a while we of AFWERX encountered some great "Yes, if..." people and agencies whose mindset of finding a way was also accompanied by an appropriate sense of urgency. This was a powerful lesson learned, and one of the key *Environment* factors for which you should scan. AFWERX did not have full-time allies on all of the review teams during our beginnings, and as a result, we were not as effective as we could have been. With time, we obtained greater legal, contracting and acquisition support from those who could see with "Yes if..." and "Yes and..." eyes.

INCREASING POSITIVE FLOW WITHIN YOUR ENVIRONMENT

Our ability to create and see beyond the present moment is one of our most advanced capabilities as humans, and creating models is one way to improve our analytic and predictive capabilities. Not everything can be easily measured by statistical analysis, especially things as hidden as a person's inner motivations or *will*. However, our *FLOW* model provides an initial, general understanding of the many external factors that affect our *will*, and the questions that follow will help you consider the more specific factors that affect the *will* for your effort. Reflecting upon these questions can help save you and your organization significant time and money that might otherwise be lost due to overlooked considerations and suboptimal execution. For your consideration, then:

*Project review judges can be scared by the risk of non-success. Where are there opportunities for you to message "mitigable risk" or "manageable risk" and distinguish those kinds of risk from the more general, spooky risk of inevitable failure?

Environments can be unintentionally challenging for innovative action. How might you, your supervisor, legal advisors, policymakers, contracting officers and others gain the ability to update regulations and policies to allow for uncertainty and experimentation, as well as integrate insights from innovative businesses? Are there risk-averse policies in place that will need waivers? Is that waiver request process known to everyone?

*How many meetings and project reviews need to be held in order to create, launch, execute and conclude a project? Do they need to occur on a "project by project basis?" A "monthly review of all projects basis?" What makes the most sense for your *Environment*?

*Who in your organization or external *Environment* has a view of "Try something new" as a threatening inkblot? Who has a view of "Try something new" as an inkblot of opportunity?

Who are the "Yes, if..." people? How can the "Yes, if..." people become assigned full-time or part-time to your innovation efforts?

*What is the standard comfort level with non-success that a review team of judges is operating with? Has a senior leader offered a standard (i.e., 80 percent likely to succeed) to help guide the review team's approval methods? When can there be democratic votes instead of 100 percent consensus?

*Do you have an appeal process in place if your project review judges are saying "Not yes?" It may not be a strong "No," but rather a desire not to accept responsibility for approving a decision. Do you have a senior leader who will accept responsibility for an innovation project proceeding in the event that a review team does not approve of your innovation project submission?

*Are budgets and issues such as "Continuing Resolution" disputes in Congress disruptive to your annual activities? How can you develop contracts or payment projections that will allow you to avoid slowdowns if fiscal year funds flow down too slowly?

*Is your resource provider (supervisor or higher up) aware of your innovation mission's possibilities or recent outcomes? How might you communicate those and increase your team's *will*?

*Does your organization suffer from high turnover rates of personnel? Or personnel who are so busy just trying to learn the rules that adding innovation seems merely like "work" and not an answer to a more enjoyable work *Environment*? How can you begin to change their *Environment* (i.e., policies, roles, responsibilities)?

3

MISSION AND STRATEGY:

THE FIRST RESPONSE

Question—who said:

"I have no expectation of making a hit every time I come to

bat. What I seek is the highest possible batting average, not only for myself, but for my team."

A. Ted Williams, the last Major League Baseball player to bat .400 or better in a season? Williams batted .406 in 1941.

B. Elon Musk, using baseball as a metaphor after another SpaceX Falcon 9 rocket failed to successfully land on a pad in 2015?

C. President Franklin D. Roosevelt, using baseball as a metaphor in a 1933 radio speech while explaining how the New Deal policies would combat the Great Depression?

The answer is ...

ANSWER: C. President Franklin D. Roosevelt

President Roosevelt is considered one of America's three greatest presidents of all time. His *Strategy* comments reflect his approach to the *Mission* of battling the *Environment* that was the Great Depression, which included a 25 percent unemployment rate, a drop in American industry productivity by over 30 percent and a significant loss of hope and *will* nationwide. Citizens experienced an unprecedented negative historical event caused by the simultaneous effects of people buying too much on credit, the stock market crashing and interest rates climbing.

The best Roosevelt could do was to (intelligently) swing the bat of public policy and government spending and hope to connect. As the New Deal efforts illustrate, sometimes it takes a real threat to make people want to attempt a more radical innovation agenda. No one knew exactly what to do with the lasting impacts of "Black Thursday" in 1929, but by 1933, people were ready to try something new. Although the historical record shows that unemployment in America did not return to under 10 percent until around 1941, and that much of the credit for America's recovery is attributed to all of the new production work that came from World War II, Roosevelt had made some progress and some hope was restored from his efforts...and it was just in time.

American citizens' renewed sense of confidence would be tested in 1941 by the Axis powers. Although the nations are now our allies, the then-governing structures of Germany, Italy and Japan sought to control the world back then. After the Pearl Harbor attack on December 7, 1941, America formally entered the war and co-created a *Coalition of the Willing*. On January 1, 1942, the United States, Great Britain, the Soviet Union, China and 22 other countries formed an alliance by signing the *Declaration by United Nations*. Their stated objective included "complete victory" over the Axis powers. This was an important first step, but it was only a partial answer to assembling a coalition of independently minded powers for the mission of World War II.

The Allied powers needed a unifying strategy. A mission without a strategy is like a flashlight whose beam is spread too wide—the scattered energy produces a sparse, dim glow that cannot create enough light for its user. For a brighter light, you need a tight focus. For the Allies, that focused strategy was summarized with two words: "Europe First."

Since those two words were responsible for defending and preserving democracy for us, we might marvel a bit at two of the strategy's key features--its brevity and its applicability. In an era that did not have the instant communication capability of cell phones and computers, leaders of the war effort had a pretty good idea about how their actions were to be prioritized. Those fighting in the Pacific were not supposed to take major offensive risks—that would come after Hitler was defeated.

Secure Europe first, then expect more forces to be deployed for a larger offensive in the Pacific. Europe first.

The formation and focus of the Allies give us a history-altering example of *Mission and Strategy* within our *FLOW* model. It demonstrates two key questions for this factor of analysis. For the Allies, they responded to those questions in the following way:

1. What is your organization's brief and applicable *Mission*?

Answer: Complete victory over the Axis powers.

It was not "Fight until the Axis nations withdraw to their original borders" nor "individual countries may negotiate peace." The Allies sought complete victory.

2. What is your organization's brief and applicable *Strategy*?

Answer: Europe first.

Though this was the US strategy, it would be adopted by the broader Allied powers over time.

MODERN-DAY FOCUS

The creation of AFWERX provides a more contemporary example of a government *Mission and Strategy* being developed. AFWERX was formed within the larger United States Air Force (USAF), and our *Mission and Strategy* needed to align with our larger *Environment*, namely the USAF's *Mission and Strategy*. With regard to the USAF in 2017:

1. What is your organization's brief and applicable *Mission*?

Answer: The mission of the United States Air Force is to fly, fight and win in air, space and cyberspace.

(In 2021, after the creation of the US Space Force, USAF's new mission became "...to fly, fight, and win...AirPower anytime, anywhere")

2. What is your organization's brief and applicable *Strategy*?

Answer: "Drive innovation to secure our future."

AFWERX's beginnings coincided with a new strategy enacted by the Air Force's senior leaders in 2017. Our mission was written into a four-page charter for which I was the lead author. Our charter included statements such as:

"AFWERX will serve as a catalyst to innovate, integrate and implement creative and disruptive technology options . . . and will foster a culture of innovation in Airmen."

Our charter also mentioned that we would primarily focus on projects with a six-to-18-month timeline. This was significant because there were already processes for innovating within a two-year time frame, and there was no reason to be redundant or to create a "turf war" with other organizations about various innovation projects and timelines. Amusingly, it took nine months for our charter to go from conception through review processes and to entry into the Air Force world —roughly the same amount of time it takes to bring a pregnancy to term.

As we were building the metaphorical AFWERX airplane while it was already in flight, we needed to develop our own brief and applicable mission and strategy statements at the same time. Eventually, we evolved to:

1. What is your organization's brief and applicable *Mission*?

Answer: Create a fusion of capabilities <u>who</u> connect innovators and accelerate results to create Air Force cultural and technological agility.

Yes, the grammar is questionable (the same could be said of "Europe first"), but it emphasized our people-centric mission.

Timeline details: This statement emerged from our reflections approximately four months after our initial team formed. We wanted to make innovation useful for the Air Force's members, but it took us a while to constructively articulate how we would accomplish that.

2. What is your organization's brief and applicable *Strategy*?

Answer: Empower. Innovate. Defend.

Timeline details: This statement emerged after approximately 20 months. It was difficult to find the words that flexibly, briefly and authentically reflected our strategy of empowering our Airmen and innovating for their needs. It looks deceptively simple in hindsight! Hopefully, if you reflect upon our mission and strategy statements (and the statements of other organizations), you will be able to create or modify your own sooner and save yourself development time.

AFWERX's *Mission* was often shortened to four words: "Connect innovators; accelerate results." AFWERX had a small core team that grew from five members to an average of around 30 members during our first three years, and we were a marvelous mix of government civilians, active-duty military, military reservists, National Guard members and contracted business and nonprofit talent.

Within our core team, we avoided using the more traditional command and control approach. The "ask your leader for permission to do something" model was used sparingly— perhaps only for large resourcing decisions or on particular messaging campaigns. Otherwise, AFWERX embraced a "centralized intent with decentralized execution" strategy, and after allocating most of our budget for the year to our dozen Capability Leaders, they pursued their declared objectives mostly as they saw fit.

Our Capability Leaders provided progress reports and collaborative planning talks approximately every three months during our AFWERX Common Mind gatherings. Words matter, and so these gatherings were not called "Commander's Call" or "Director's Call." Instead, Common Mind gatherings were about the "WE" of AF*WE*RX. Our Capability Leaders also joined me for one-on-one talks (that we called "pondering sessions") every two weeks, which offered additional chances to provide project updates (a more detailed description of the Capabilities our Leaders cultivated will be found in Chapter 5).

BUILDING A STRATEGY FOR UNKNOWN FUTURES

No one can consistently predict the future. How, then, do you prepare for a future that is full of unknowns and uncertainties? Many of us have already experienced a best practice answer to this question with something very personal to each of us: our "investing for retirement" strategy.

Should you ever put all of your eggs in one investment basket? No. It is far safer to invest in a broad and diverse portfolio of opportunities as a way to hedge your bets against unknown risks and future challenges. Stocks, bonds, index funds, real estate, IRAs, collectibles and more make up a "risk-hedging" strategy, because a wide variety of approaches usually yields better average growth and financial returns over the long term. Placing all of your money into just one type of investment typically adds *Environment* risk. For example, if you invest only in umbrellas and it is a dry year, your singular focus will cost you—and you will thirst for a more diversified approach to investing.

The strategy of diversification extends beyond personal finance to areas as broad as national defense. For example, the Air Force has a diverse range of aircraft ready to respond to different challenges—bigger planes for holding bombs, smaller tactical fighter aircraft for fast attack impacts and so on. Similarly, and on a larger scale, the Department of Defense has a diverse approach to defending American interests with an Army, Navy, Marine Corps, Air Force, Coast Guard and, most recently, a Space Force.

The same was true of AFWERX's approach to innovation. We used multiple approaches to innovation that would cover the spectrum of Air Force demands, from innovations for individual airmen to projects with Air Force-wide impact. As the previous graphic reminds us, if you only have a hammer then everything looks like a nail and you can only push, pound and move around your objective. By contrast, if your strategy includes developing multiple tools and skills for the challenges you face, then you can build strong houses from your multi-tool mastery.

THINK BIG, START SMALL, FAIL CHEAP, LEARN FAST, WIN BIG (AT SCALE)

There is a shorter version of the above heading. It is expressed as "Think Big. Start Small. Scale Fast." That statement can be deceptive, because it does not state the critical issue of failure and how you should view and message it.

Much like the batting average quote from President Franklin D. Roosevelt, innovation requires taking experimental swings at a number of projects and approaches, not all of which will be successful. The key is your average impact. Written slightly differently and without the baseball jargon:

A successful innovation effort invests in a number of small bets across a broad portfolio of initiatives and then achieves a "net benefit" result by having the bigger, positive outcomes outweigh the costs of the little failures (which are likely more numerous).

Within a successful innovation effort, on average and over time, the fewer, bigger wins will outweigh the smaller, cheaper non-successes. Thus, the average effect of the cost of non-success compared to the benefit of success leads to a long-term "net benefit" from the greater, positive impacts.

Our language describes and creates our realities, and message articulation matters even more when talking about emotionally negative things such as "failure" and "risk." Remember, "failure" is only failure if you do not learn from it. Ideally, the little failures will become cheap "lessons learned" that provide faster learning curves and better iterations in future efforts. Failure can be incredibly cheap in pursuit of a "net benefit" average.

For example, suppose that you strategically send out a targeted email to 100 technology companies. It is a targeted email query because you intelligently scanned your database (or asked a talented partner to scan their databases) and you believe that these companies have already built or could build the kind of technology you are seeking. If only 15 companies respond to your email query, does that mean that you had an 85 percent failure rate from your effort? Alternatively, does it mean that your cheap experiment yielded 15 new leads from which you can take a multiple-path approach to finding a competitively priced technology? The "net benefit" effect will appear as the fewer wins with bigger technology impact outweigh the cheap cost of email non-responses, even if the raw scorecard of your effort looks like "15 wins, 85 non-wins." The magnitude of benefit and costs matters.

AFWERX had its share of cheap non-successes during our startup years. For example, we canceled a monthly "First Friday" community gathering event after the crowds diminished to a point where it no longer seemed worth the effort. We also stopped using software packages if they did not seem to be worth the cost. Within AFWERX, there was no giant "all eggs in one basket" initiative to which we were beholden. If some process or product was not working as expected and we had taken reasonable measures to try and adjust it, then we eliminated the effort, learned and moved on.

Many leaders, resource providers and approving authorities did not like to hear the phrase "Fail fast."

"Beam, are you telling me that you are going to deliberately fail?"

No, not deliberately—unavoidably. No set of experiments will be 100 percent effective 100 percent of the time. Nonsuccess is inevitable but it can be cheap and the learning from it can be valuable and rapid. The rapid journey towards effective innovation on a small scale—often called a "minimum viable product"—helps create a much more effective end-result when you increase the scaling of your prototype into a mainstream product, policy or culture capability.

HAVE THE WILL TO LEARN FROM FAILURE AND MOVE ON

The ability to view failure as a learning opportunity and press on, however disappointing, is a major test of our *will*. What did Thomas Edison think after his 500th "failure" in his pursuit of the light bulb? What about after failure number 1000? 2000? What kind of inner drive and morale must he and his team have possessed? We do have some idea. An interviewer once asked Edison about all of the experiments he had performed that had not led to any results. Edison's reply included a smile as he said, "Results?! Why, man, I have gotten lots of results! I know several thousand things that won't work!"

What kind of *will* must Franklin Roosevelt have possessed? Much of the New Deal did not work and recovery from the Great Depression took over a decade. As retold in Burton Folsom's book *New Deal or Raw Deal?*, Treasury Secretary

Henry Morgenthau Jr. told his fellow Democrats on the House Ways and Means Committee in 1939:

> "We have tried spending money. We are spending money more than we have ever spent before and it does not work. And I have just one interest, and if I am wrong...somebody else can have my job. I want to see this country prosperous. I want to see people get a job. I want to see people get enough to eat. We have never made good on our promises...I say after eight years of this Administration we have just as much unemployment as when we started...and an enormous debt to boot!"

Ultimately, it took the employment and earnings increases associated with wartime production for World War II to bring the United States citizenry out of their depressed economic status. However, the optimist in me would like to believe that had World War II not occurred, the "batting average" of the multiple program approach used by the Roosevelt administration would have eventually brought about enough lessons and insights to focus the New Deal initiatives into increasingly more useful recovery efforts. Whether it is national poverty or creating light bulbs, the following sage advice for dealing with "failure" still holds true:

THE ONLY ANTIDOTE
TO SUFFERING

IS EFFORT

@gapingvoid

TRANSFORMING STRATEGIC THEORY INTO PRACTICE WITH OKRs

Four times per year, AFWERX deliberately paused to gather our nationally dispersed team (typically, we operated from nine different locations) and reflect upon where we had traveled, where we were and where we might next go. At these Common Mind gatherings, we devoted a significant portion of our time to identifying and recording our progress with Objectives and Key Results (OKRs).

Andy Grove first developed OKRs as a way of focusing efforts with objectives, and the approach has been used by companies such as Google, Amazon and LinkedIn. The system is rather simple, like so many useful things. It begins with the leader (or committee or organization) setting the big-picture objectives. For AFWERX, we created three overarching objectives for our initial year, and they endured through our startup years:

1. Develop and implement capabilities to increase warfighter agility.
2. Unleash airmen innovation capability—anytime, anywhere.
3. Create and leverage an engaged, possibility-expanding ecosystem.

Our dozen Capability Leaders then established how their Capability's efforts would support those common, overarching objectives. For example, for fiscal year 2020, we created a spreadsheet like the one below. Capability leaders filled in their three-statements-or-less answers to each question, and would then brief our whole Common Mind attendance on their answers during our in-person or virtual gatherings:

Capability Leader Link to Overarching Goals

1. What is the estimated number of selected prototypes, completed prototypes and prototypes-in-process that my Capability will contribute to the DoD as of 30 Sep 2020?

2. How is my Capability contributing to unleashing Airmen innovation "anytime and anywhere," with elaboration of estimated capability by 30 Sep 2020? (educated guesses welcomed)

3. How is my Capability contributing to, creating and leveraging a well-connected, well-engaged, possibility-expanding ecosystem?

Not every AFWERX Capability was expected to support all three goals. For example, we did not expect Marketing and Public Affairs to complete any prototype projects, but we certainly expected that talented team to increase AFWERX's connectivity and ecosystem engagement with the broader community. Of course, if your organization has placed resources in a Capability that cannot answer any of your overarching goal questions, then you should consider creating an additional "overarching" goal that the Capability Leader is pursuing. Otherwise, you could eliminate that Capability effort and reallocate the associated resources to efforts that do support your overarching goals.

With the overarching goals in place, the next table that each Capability Leader filled out was typically three objectives and three key results that showed how they were supporting one, two or three of our overarching goals. An example of an OKR table for a Capability Leader with regard to the first overarching objective would be:

Objective #1: Number of Prototypes	Minimum Viable Result	FY20 Update or Final
Measurable Key Result #1	23 widgets from effort A	
Measurable Key Result #2	16 gadgets from effort B	
Measurable Key Result #3	12 cogs from effort C	

Capability Leaders would be responsible for discussing their rationale for MVR targets during Common Mind gatherings. AFWERX members might then ask questions about the assumptions that went into the rationale. Projections of estimated results, or even the objective itself, might then be modified.

A few other thoughts on OKRs:

- There was no magic formula for whether a Capability should have more or less than three objectives. However, there was evidence that three OKRs allowed for a Capability Leader to show the variety of their efforts without having to make up "bovine feces" just to fill four or five blocks worth of OKRs.

- An Objective was typically a sentence or phrase (less than 15 words).
- A measurable KR typically ranged from a phrase to three sentences, often less than 30 words in length.
- The Minimum Viable Result (MVR) was based on an 80-85 percent outcome estimated within a relatively stable *Environment* (i.e., steady resources, no pandemics).
- We tried adding "Audacious Goals" as a column, but it was not taken seriously. We might have gained better responses with a framing of "Assume a perfect *Environment...*"
- After our first two rounds of OKR goal-setting and updating, it took less than six hours per quarter to fill out these charts. After all, these were the key foci of each Capability Leader's efforts, so the information was more of an input exercise than it was a deep research and reflection process. Light, agile reporting allowed more time to be devoted to innovation.

Some organizations like to make OKR goal-setting sessions a quarterly affair. We set year-long OKRs and used our quarterly gatherings to highlight progress and trouble areas where we could use help. One of the advantages of a year-long OKR system was that it matched up nicely with government reporting and resourcing cycles, which helped shape our progress reports to the senior leaders who resourced us. Depending upon how much time your wish to devote to generating reports, you could pursue monthly OKR sessions. At the extreme, you could perform daily or hourly OKRs, but surely there is a point where there is too much reporting.

Not only can the OKR review be a source of collective pride as you share your empowerment successes publicly, it can also offer a bit of fun and reveal the individual character of your team members. For example, as a final input table for each Capability Leader within AFWERX, we might create bonus questions such as "What picture best represents your Capability's OKRs?" or "What superhero, Greek or Roman god or Aesop's fable is most like your Capability?" Simple questions about people's preferences and reflections helped support team camaraderie through easy-going, low-effort bonding experiences that highlighted some of the essence of our talented team.

WHEN REALITY BREAKS DOWN THE *FLOW* SEQUENCE

It can be tempting to jump around the various factors and layers within the *FLOW* model. It may also be necessary. For example, you may already know who your team members will be and your initial budget. There is nothing "wrong" with possessing that knowledge ahead of the *FLOW* model sequence. However, starting to answer those kinds of *Input and Processes* factor questions too soon before considering factors such as *Culture* and *Structure,* can lead to out-of-sequence mistakes that result in lost time later. Why limit your scanning and brainstorming prematurely?

Within AFWERX, we may have been less strategic during the controlled chaos of our beginnings. Rather than having an initial mind-expanding series of gatherings to explore the art of the possible within an ideal *Environment*, we were probably a little quick to say, "These are our people and resources; let's get started." As a team of military members or former military members, we were influenced by then-Secretary of Defense Donald Rumsfeld's comments in 2004: "You go to war with the army you have, not the army you might want or wish to have at a later time."

The tradeoffs between speed, quality and cost are an endless series of calculations. With hindsight, there was probably time for a little better conceptualization of our mission, strategy and resourcing. Then again, too much thinking and overthinking can lead to inaction and paralysis by analysis. Since there was no blueprint for how to build an innovation system for a 680,000-person organization, we decided to use a strategy that would build upon our individual and collective strengths. We hypothesized that we would eventually grow into a cohesive *Supply and Demand* structure that we will exhibit and explore in Chapter 5. We would also leverage Abraham Maslow's "self-actualization" insights at an organizational level, as we will demonstrate in Chapter 6. Our first year was gritty, but by 2020, we had experimented our way into a relatively stable and effective innovation system with a clear *Mission and Strategy*.

Lastly, it would be incomplete to explore *Mission and Strategy* as they relate to innovation without also mentioning the natural complement to all of this activity: designating time for rest and reflection. No matter how strong your *will* is, it is still contained within a material body—and bodies need rest.

At a meta-level, nature offers us a guide for rest. Before a season of new beginnings (spring), and after a season of high performance and heat (summer), there is a season of slow down (fall) and rest (winter). Body-fitness efforts also provide us with similar clues. It is rare to exercise the exact same muscle groups two days in a row. Even marathon athletes who are seemingly always running will add in high-speed sprint work-outs for their legs' fast-twitch muscles as a bit of rest and in complement to their longer endurance workouts.

The act of innovation is an exciting, engrossing and energy-demanding endeavor. To effectively persist within innovation, harmony between hard work and recovery is essential. AFWERX had its Common Mind gatherings, but we still needed to remind one another to schedule time away from our mission activities for vacations or long weekends. With rest and recovery, we emerge stronger and increase our longevity. Please remember to take care of yourself and your fellow innovators as you perform your mission!

INCREASING POSITIVE FLOW WITHIN MISSION AND STRATEGY

*What is your organization's simple, brief and applicable guiding innovation mission statement?

*What is your organization's simple, brief and applicable guiding innovation strategy?

*How does your organization's *Mission and Strategy* align with the larger and nearer *Environments* of the organization providing you resources?

*Are there other organizations that might view your innovation efforts as a competitor? Are there other organizations that might view you as an ally or complementary effort? Are there any "turf wars" for resources that could be associated with your effort? How can you begin meeting with these organizations' members to create a friendlier, collaborative *Environment* for all?

*Do your stakeholders understand the "lessons learned" aspect of experimental innovation and that there are many nuances to "failure" and "non-failure?" How is it being messaged?

*How are you pursuing a multiple-effort approach to innovation (i.e., by capability, by region, by in-person versus digital media)? How are you avoiding the higher risk associated with having "all eggs in one basket?" If you are using a diversified portfolio approach, are you messaging the "net benefit" aspects of innovation where the magnitude of effect matters more than the raw success vs. non-success numbers?

*Do your leaders have the right mindset and support for your effort (i.e., your innovation effort might not be an overnight success and many cheap failures are possible)?

*Do you have a senior leader or other resource-allocating authority supporting your organization via a formal government charter, or some other declarative statement or budget allocation?

*Do you have overarching OKRs or other measuring methods

to highlight your progress? Were they created in a manner that made everyone on your team feel like they were a part of the process? Do they engage ownership of their Capability as a result?

*How are your OKRs being monitored and supported? What kinds of data about non-aligned activities might cause you to consider reallocating resources or adjusting your measurements?

*How are you establishing times for reflection, strategic thinking and rest for your innovation team members?

4

CULTURE:

THE UNSEEN ENGINE

Once upon a time, the most renowned military mind in all of China, Sun Tzu, was visiting a king at his courtyard where a large crowd had assembled. The king, who was not easily impressed by others' reputations, especially when the others were not kings, decided to put Sun Tzu to a test.

"Master Sun," began the king, "do you think you can train my concubines?"

"We are all capable of excellence, your Highness," replied Sun Tzu. "Please send me 202 of your favorite ladies and I shall begin training them now."

The king had his servants escort 202 of his concubines to a large area in front of his throne. Sun Tzu divided them into two groups of 100 ladies, arranged them into 10 x 10 formations and placed the remaining two ladies at the front of each group.

"You two are the leaders of these groups," Sun Tzu said as he pointed his sword at the front two ladies. Then, in a louder voice, he said to all of the women: "The king would like you to be trained for warfare."

The front two ladies giggled a bit and looked at each other and their groups, who were also snickering.

"You are now all facing forward," Sun Tzu began with a voice that filled the courtyard, "and when I say 'Turn right,' you will turn 90 degrees to your right. Turn, right!"

The concubines looked at each other with amusement and then burst out laughing.

Sun Tzu looked away from the ladies and spoke to the king. "Your Highness, when your troops do not perform as you expect, it is possible that there has been a miscommunication."

Sun Tzu looked back at the ladies and said, "Ladies, and leaders, do you each know which way is your right and which is your left?"

The ladies nodded their heads lazily.

Sun Tzu then asked, "And does everyone here know how to turn right and left?"

Again, the ladies rolled their eyes and acknowledged that they did.

"Very well, let us try this one more time," Sun Tzu said, his voice rising. "Turn, right!"

The ladies once again began laughing, placing their heads upon one another's shoulders and wiping tears from their eyes. *Whoooooooosh! Slash! Foooooooosh! Slash!* Sun Tzu launched himself at the two front ladies and promptly cut off their heads! All of the concubines froze in place, their faces showing a mix of horror, disbelief and fear.

"You two," Sun Tzu calmly said as he picked another lady from each of the groups. "Come, stand where your prior leaders were once standing."

The ladies quickly and quietly ran to their newly appointed leadership positions.

"Turn, right!" Sun Tzu commanded.

Two-hundred concubines turned to their right, silently.

"Turn, left!!" Sun Tzu commanded.

Two-hundred concubines turned left and faced forward, silently.

"You see, your Majesty," beamed Sun Tzu. "In the lethal arts, when the leader gives an order, and the troops all understand the order, there can be no hesitation or else the whole unit will become vulnerable. It is the leaders' job to make sure that their troops follow the orders of the commanding general. If the orders are clear and the troops are capable of performing the order, then it is the leaders' fault if the orders are not performed. We are all capable of excellence, even in lethal affairs. Some people just need more incentive to focus than others."

Question: On the basis of this story, do you have a sense of what it would have been like to be in Sun Tzu's army? For example, what level of importance did Sun Tzu place upon discipline—"high" or "low?" Were you able to come to this conclusion even though you have never seen a mission statement or a strategy document from the army of Sun Tzu?

THE UNSEEN ENGINE

Culture—the values, norms, beliefs, customs and processes of an organization that impact its members' experiences and behavior—is the next factor affecting organizational *will*.

When you are an outsider to an organization, the organization's *Mission and Strategy* are often more easily observed than the *Culture*. You might even be able to find another organization's *Mission and Strategy* posted on a website. However, an organization's *Culture*, which powers all of the efforts to move together in a common direction, will not be so easily found as a visible artifact. An organization's *Culture* should flow in alignment with *Mission and Strategy*. Culture should not be an afterthought or be given no thought at all, or else the best *Mission and Strategy* will break apart into disharmony.

There is no single, perfect *Culture* that will fit all organizations. For example, some companies have a "turn and burn"

Culture, where it is expected that people will be hired, work like mad for 80-100 hours per week and make themselves and the company crazy rich. Investment firms and more than a few consultancies in the private sector acknowledge that they will have a high turnover rate, with people leaving after three to five years tired but wealthy. Other firms have a more stable operation, such as manufacturing plants that are based on eight to 10 hours of shift work five days a week. Their *Culture* has far fewer surprises and far fewer 50+ hour work weeks accompanying their *Environment*, and the pay is often more modest than "turn and burn" *Cultures*. Successful *Cultures* can be quite different, much like the people who choose to work within them.

Government innovation offers a unique hybrid of *Cultures*. It appeals to the creative, work-crazy-hours spirit of many creative people. At the same time, no one is going to get rich from leading government innovation efforts, so incentives such as interesting work, patriotic fulfillment and great teammates are often part of the effort's "pay" and compensation. Government also comes with a large set of regulations to navigate, which can either be useful, protective guidance or an outdated obstacle that requires updating.

Whether in government or the private sector, an energizing *Culture* is the result of intentional design, constant monitoring and a willingness to adjust if the organization is not living up to its *Mission and Strategy* (a review of the OKRs may also be needed). Ignoring *Culture* will leave an innovation effort and its organization subject to the forces of entropy and atrophy, causing the organization's *will* to fade into mechanical, contracted exchanges of working for pay but not for personal fulfillment.

Organizations should be as transparent as possible about their *Cultures* to boost their members' collective *will*. Whenever possible, job seekers choose organizations that are compatible with their preferred *Culture*. For that reason, recruiters should make sure that their descriptions of their organization's *Culture* match the impressions of frontline innovators and perhaps even outside observers. If the descriptions are not relatively similar, then new recruits will not have the consistent *Culture* they need to make informed decisions about their longevity at a given organization. That inconsistency between expectations and reality can result in high turnover, leaving the organization with unfilled positions and missed opportunities to have hired people who would have been a better fit.

Culture is also why members of an organization get nervous when a new leader takes control. The new leader may not value the previous *Culture*, and that previous *Culture* may have been a crucial reason why people joined the organization. There are many ways a leader can affect a *Culture* and some of them are included in this Top 10, presented in no particular order of importance:

1. Changing the mission, strategy or Objectives & Key Results (OKRs).
2. Changing the metrics that measure and reward OKR productivity.
3. Changing the frequency of daily or weekly reporting or changing the format of that reporting (from a verbal form to a more time-consuming written form, for example).
4. Changing members' job roles and responsibilities.
5. Changing the organization's information transparency and sharing.
6. Changing members' workloads without increasing their resources to do the work.
7. Changing the type of decisions requiring the new leader's approval.
8. Changing subordinates' plans without asking the subordinates for their input.
9. Changing the standards for what qualifies as passable work

on various administrative tasks—not all tasks are equally important.

10. Changing from a culture of collaborative "asking" to top-down "tasking" as leaders tell subordinates what to do.

ARTICULATING CULTURE

In 2018, I was listening to a presentation from *Culture* expert Jason Korman of Gapingvoid when he asked:

> *"If I were to randomly select five people from your organization and ask them to describe your organization's Culture, how similar do you think their comments would be?"*

Jason's question sent my mind racing. I was about one month away from our team's first "in-person" Common Mind gathering of everyone from AFWERX (we began as a geographically separated team in six different locations), and I wanted to articulate an easily understood *Culture* model that reflected our innovative "action for impact" spirit.

I developed the following *W.A.T.E.R. Culture* standard that I promised to defend for our AFWERX Talent. I offered that anyone was invited to use this *W.A.T.E.R.* standard to bring concerns to me if they thought one of my actions or decisions went against this *Culture.* Similarly, I would expect that we conduct ourselves with a *W.A.T.E.R.* mindset of fluidity and agility in thought and action. I referenced this model at every quarterly Common Mind meeting, typically with fun associations such as how *Culture* has a *Star Wars* Force-like quality ("*Culture* surrounds us, penetrates us and binds the galaxy together"). Over time, we even started performing magic tricks during our *W.A.T.E.R.* discussions, further reflecting *Culture's* fascinating, Force-like effects.

Our *W.A.T.E.R. Culture* reflected how AFWERX was:

W: Warfighter-focused. Any successful innovation effort and organization should have the end-users of customers (and collaborators of) its products in mind while iterating prototypes. For AFWERX, our end-users were the warfighters. The warfighters' needs were our #1 guiding priority. If any AFWERX members' actions would not be in service of producing greater capability for our nation's defenders, then those actions should not be performed.

A: Agile and Autonomous. Creating options at the speed of relevance is both a cultural mindset and a structural consideration. For example, when we started AFWERX, we held two mandatory hour-long meetings for our nationally dispersed team each week. Over time, we felt it was not the most effective forum and so we switched that meeting to a frequency of just one per month. During that 90-minute meeting, each Capability Leader reported on their most important efforts from the previous month, current month and upcoming month. Seven extra afternoons of flexibility were gained each month because of this change.

We also aimed for minimal weekly reporting and other bureaucratic oversight. Wherever possible, we sought to allow our front-line innovators, in collaboration with our end-users, to make the decisions necessary to execute their part of their mission—rarely were generals or senior executives involved in our decisions. This helped keep our development speed faster and avoided the dangerous time trap of too many senior-level reviews.

We were able to maintain this agile environment because of some great senior leaders, such as Air Force Vice Chief of Staff Gen Stephen "Seve" Wilson, who said during a Town Hall meeting in July 2020:

> *"I was reflecting upon our first three years of starting AFWERX and about how I never once asked Beam and team to perform any specific task by a specific date. I only said to AFWERX, 'Drive on! Drive Innovation to secure our future' and they delivered again and again..."*

T: True to our core. A popular saying often attributed to Albert Einstein is: "If you cannot explain it simply, you do not understand it well." Within AFWERX, the four words "Connect innovators; accelerate results" reflected our core *Mission* as simply as possible. If we were not connecting or accelerating to some warfighter's benefit, then we were not being true to our cause.

E: Empowered Talent. A key ingredient to our AFWERX team was empowered and educated Talent. You would not hand over a multi-million-dollar Air Force aircraft to someone who has never flown and say, "Go fly that." Similarly, you would not start an Air Force-wide innovation system by picking people at random and saying, "Go drive innovation."

AFWERX had the good fortune of starting with talented innovators whose training and experiences supported their ability to empower others to "get stuff done." Our Talent moved with agility because we had studied or practiced with innovation frameworks such as Design Thinking, Lean Design and Appreciative Inquiry. With this educated Talent, it was possible to credibly execute our strategy of centralized intent (from our Common Mind OKRs) with decentralized execution by our Capability Leaders and other talented members. Although OKRs were scheduled to be updated approximately every three months, sometimes we skipped an OKR update due to other *Environment* priorities such as during the COVID outbreak. Yet the mission still carried on, due to our empowered Talent performing decentralized execution.

R: Relationship-Building. The "official" core membership of AFWERX resided in about a dozen government personnel slots, but AFWERX had over 30 military, business and nonprofit members supporting our mission on a full-time basis. By our third year, we had over 150 members who contributed part-time and full-time to various innovation projects.

We sought to create win-win opportunities for those who joined us to work on projects, and thus AFWERX did not force projects upon organizations. It was through friendly, transparent and hard-working team actions that our innovations advanced. The resulting camaraderie and trust built through that process created a powerful *Culture* of solid relationships and effective efforts. This sometimes meant turning down projects or reducing relationships when the efforts and energy that we expended did not appear to be reciprocated by others. AFWERX did not seek a certain quantity of individuals or projects to reflect our relationship strength; instead, we sought a quality of Talent who valued and helped scale the impact of our efforts for the warfighter.

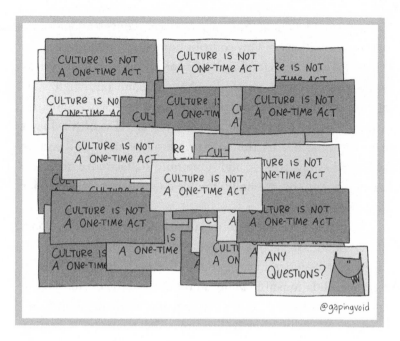

@gapingvoid

MULTIPLE CONSISTENT *CULTURE* METHODS

What follows are some of the many visible components from AFWERX's cornucopia of *Culture*—emails, processes, artifacts and more:

Email can reflect Culture

Our language constructs our reality or limits it. For example, whether you speak of yourself as holding a "pro-life" or "pro-choice" perspective implies two very different interpretations of what matters most to you for a particular situation. The words used in emails, memos and newsletters are also very visible reflections of your interpretation and contribution to your *Culture*.

Some members will use email strictly for asking or tasking. I believed that the Relationship-building within our *W.A.T.E.R.*

Culture would benefit from a consistent, conversational tone and personality within my contribution of communiques. Since AFWERX was a geographically dispersed mission team, weeks could pass before I physically saw someone (although VTC offered significant connectivity). Informed by science and art, I committed to communicating with all of AFWERX's Talent with a special header (for ease of reference and email sorting later) and always tried to add something—a factoid, a historical reference and occasionally humor—to further connect our dispersed Talent.

At first, not everyone appreciated these longer emails. Some of our Talent asked (very respectfully) if I could get to the point of my email sooner. I accepted that feedback as a testament to our open Relationship *Culture*, and I evolved the emails to have an *** Action Items *** summary portion at the beginning and used an *** Additional Background and Context *** section afterward for elaboration for those who wanted to learn more. A typical email might look something like the one I sent just before Memorial Day weekend in 2020:

Subject: FOR AFWERX...FOR AFWERX...before the Rah Rah, it was Rah-kets' Red Glare...

Dear Diverse Talent within our Common Mind,

*** ACTION ITEMS ***

a. Part of the reason that you can read this email is because people who never met you died defending the democracy that you now live within—please honor Memorial Day with spirit and or action.

b. The updated AFWERX 101 Slides are located in the Common Mind folder on the shared drives.

c. Gentle Reminder: If you want to keep using G-Suite, you must fill out the quick form—find your email titled "ACTION: New Terms of Use Form for All Users"

*** ADDITIONAL BACKGROUND AND CONTEXT ***

Many colleges and high schools have a fight song that is played during sports competitions. In America, we rise above even the most intense rivalries—temporarily—to rise for our National Anthem. "The Star-Spangled Banner" (first known as "The Defense of Fort McHenry") is a fight song from the War of 1812. Amazingly, it took over 100 years for the popular song to finally be sanctioned by President Wilson and Congress.

Although some of us were required to memorize all five verses for boot camp, most Americans are only aware of the first verse, and so for the knowledge opportunity, attached is a link to "the rest of the story."

Our language constructs our realities, and so we must guard our words against simply calling the next few days "a long weekend." Every generation of civilization has its share of aggressors, whether Attila the Hun or Adolf Hitler. Weakness provokes aggressors to action. Strength deters. What you do every day increases America's agility and deterrence capabilities.

Thank you for being You.

AFX-5 out... Tuebor...

Yes, an email like that took more time, but the cost of the extra 15 minutes to look up a fact or two was part of a broad portfolio of *Culture* investments designed to create a longer-term benefit of a unified *Culture* designed to support a *Mission and Strategy* in response to our *Environment*. I received significant positive feedback for my lengthier emails, including a fun example from a part-time project contributor. I had never met him before, but at an AFWERX event he approached me and said, "When I need to reflect on life and think deep thoughts, I just pop open a bottle of wine and read some of your old emails." The little "educate and entertain" moments in an email can contribute to a *Culture*.

What is the one Culture *goal that most, if not all, people should have in common?*

As part of his writings in *The Nicomachean Ethics*, Aristotle was one of the first people to answer the common-goal question. Well over 2,000 years ago, Aristotle noted that people perform most activities merely as steps to a final, common destination. More specifically, most people engage in activities that they believe will ultimately make them reach a final status of "Happiness."

People do not pursue activities that they perceive will lead them to a worse position in life. Instead, someone might give up personal time in favor of work to earn money. However, earning money is not the person's final goal—earning money is only a step towards buying an object or an experience...and why? Because the buyer believes that the object (e.g., a new vehicle) or the experience (e.g., a vacation or visit with family) will make them happier.

Aristotle's insight on happiness is part of a broader triangulation of how a motivating *Culture* will support purpose, fulfillment and happiness. Not all three criteria must be met at once. Many people are willing to endure periods of non-happiness—such as neutral or even negative overtime hours and sacrifice—for a higher purpose. Additionally, fulfillment may not always be a steady feeling because people usually do not feel fulfilled while pursuing the completion of some project or task. However, a motivating *Culture* is one that will offer a credible shot at staying in the triangulated area of Purpose-Happiness-Fulfillment time and time again. No one stays on target permanently. Change happens. *Environment* happens. New goals emerge.

As a member of a government organization, you have an incredible opportunity to tap into this triangulation of motivation. People voluntarily choose to work at government organizations such as the Treasury Department, the State Department or the US Forest Service, so there must have been something about those organizations' *Mission and Culture* that was appealing. Perhaps it was keeping the economy running, advancing worldwide diplomacy or perhaps making our nation's forests and grasslands capable of meeting the needs of present and future generations. It is useful for government members to understand and authentically feel the links of their efforts to the triangle. Target the triangle!

Triangulation with W.A.T.E.R., even during a pandemic

When COVID-19 took the United States to a condition of "shelter in place," we were very deliberate about searching for additional insights on Happiness and Resilience, and we composed emails to AFWERX with a more life-centric "entertain and education" tone. An excerpt from one of those emails is as follows:

Dear Diverse Talent within Our Common Mind,

First, I hope that this message reaches you each in good health. Our various data sources show that our collective Talent is generally of good physical health, but please remember that your spiritual health at the Hotel Happy is found via the larger destination located at the "Community by the **SEA.**" *[An explanation of the phrasing follows]*

Community: Being connected to others...it need not be "many" others, but a "connection" with a friend, family member or a work colleague can do wonders to enhance the positive and mitigate against negatives.

Sleep: It is generally easier to be happy with seven to eight hours of rest than five to six hours.

Exercise: An elevated heart rate (not a mad dash/frenzied/about-to-collapse workout) for 30 minutes, three times per week can also enhance our well-being. Data show people are typically happier when they are exercising.

Achievement: Whether for professional achievement or personal, non-paid interest (it is nice when the two overlap), authentic growth (which includes challenges) is shown to be linked with a happier life. I believe we all can agree that AFWERX offers plenty of challenge and a chance for growth as we create new realities.

...and since this is a non-ordinary time, our extraordinary opportunity of our Virtual AFWERX Community gathering (Common Mind) will have the following agenda:

__ Greetings from Beam
__ Instead of OKR review:
__ Reflections for virtual Common Mind—practice a two-minute pitch with:

1. Find a photo of who you are fighting to protect via AFWERX —family, friends, Whiskers, Rover, etc.

2. Retrieve a favorite quote or landscape or picture that inspires you.

...but Beam, I understand why people may matter for Happiness and Purpose, what is the point of this non-people exploration?

Thanks for asking! It turns out that moments of "awe" and "wonder" also provide us with a sense of "Commune-ing" with something greater than ourselves...and that can be linked to a happier, more fulfilling existence for us.

___ I will send out the link for posting photos later in the week.

Our mission continues, fluid and agile, in response to the challenges of the day...and the future...AFX-5 out...with optimistic anticipation...

Yes, that kind of happiness and resiliency research took more than a few minutes to find, yet it seemed worth it for our people and it had positive effects for our *Culture* and camaraderie.

Such lengthy emails may not be needed if your entire team is in the same office or meets regularly through virtual means. Maybe physical proximity and time zone sameness help aid camaraderie and emails can be replaced with in-person or virtual conversations. However, if your team is spread across multiple time zones and you only gather once or so per month, then weekly emails or recorded videos will likely offer you *Culture*-contributing communication opportunities.

Magic show, anyone?

Our first AFWERX Common Mind gathering included an optional dinner and a magic show outing (personal expense, not government or taxpayer-paid). Intentional planning for shared experiences beyond project work boosted our camaraderie and our *Culture*.

Call signs and mission coins

After six months, an AFWERX member was eligible for a military "call sign" nickname, nominated and selected by the attending group Common Mind Talent. The call sign was not used all of the time, but it further reinforced our connection to a military mission. The newly named Talent for our team also received a mission coin at that time, which looked like:

@gapingvoid

Lead with ideas, not rank

We did not use rank or titles on our AFWERX team. This was rather unusual for a military organization, but we believed that it helped the better ideas rise to the top and make group discussions less prone to rank bias.

Culture change includes creating alternate reality-thoughts and legendary stories

We created a "lessons learned" and "best practices" insights ebook, which can be found online or searched with keywords: *AFWERX: Empowering Next Generation Innovators and Innovations.*

Investing in organizational self-reflection beyond thoughts

We also created our own *CHRONICLES OF AFWERX* book after 18 months—something similar to a high school yearbook and a way to honor and reflect upon our past, present and future.

INCREASING POSITIVE FLOW WITHIN CULTURE

*How does your organization visibly show what is valued
with its:
—Mission, strategy and OKRs
—Metrics that measure OKR productivity (and awards and
compensation that an individual may receive)
—Daily or weekly reporting, whether in verbal or written form
—Job roles and responsibilities of members
—Organizational transparency and access to information
—Resource allocations to organizational workloads
undertaken
—Decisions requiring the additional approvals beyond the
frontline innovators
—Changing of plans with or without asking for frontline inno-
vators' inputs
—Standards for what qualifies as passable work on various
administrative tasks
—The amount of collaborative "asking" vs. top-down "tasking"

*Can you articulate your organization's *Culture*? Do you think
four other randomly-picked people from your organization
would offer a similar description of the *Culture*?

*For whom are you innovating? Who are your end-users? How
do you support and add value to your collaborative partners?

*How much bureaucratic review and how many mandatory
meetings do you have for your whole organization (gentle
reminder: a full team meeting likely has a lot of components
that are not value-adding to every individual's time)?

*Does your team possess the knowledge skills and abilities so
that you can empower them and increase your innovation
speed? If not, how might you develop their skills?

*What is your common communication and coordination strategy? For example, do you have digital document sharing and project event calendars that your whole team can see?

*How do your meetings, emails, memos, newsletters and social media campaigns reflect your *Culture*?

*Government service is service. Members take an oath to defend the Constitution. How might you incorporate that into your government organization's *Culture*? What could you do—such as emails that reflect upon our nation's history—to remind your team of their higher purpose in government service and their contribution to a national impact? What are other government "pays" for the service citizens offer?

5

STRUCTURE:

FLIPPING SUPPLY AND DEMAND

One of the most influential structure paradigms for AFWERX may be traced back to an article by Tom Goodwin, published by TechCrunch.com in 2015. Tom noticed that:

"Uber, the world's largest taxi company, owns no
vehicles.
Facebook, the world's most popular media owner,
creates no content.
Alibaba, the most valuable retailer, has no inventory.
And Airbnb, the world's largest accommodation
provider, owns no real estate.
Something interesting is happening."

Something interesting had happened, indeed. World-impacting companies were offering goods and services without owning the actual things consumers desired. These companies were connectors linking consumer demand with a supply of options.

AFWERX began with a goal of connecting "customers"—individual or multiple airmen—with idea-to-prototype development capabilities (sometimes called "ideation" capabilities). We did not own any production lines. We also did not own any funding for the prototype projects. Our value came from our connectivity and in empowering those with whom we connected.

In the beginning, we had to resist a large messaging push by a number of people who wanted us to describe how AFWERX worked by using some kind of neural network, Artificial Intelligence simile. They reasoned that innovation seemed a little bit mysterious, with lots of outcomes occurring because of connections and activities that were outside of most people's direct view and control. The "out-of-sight actions lead to results" approach, it was argued, could be perceived like AI algorithms at work. That neural network concept had some merit, but others of us thought it made AFWERX sound like a random process.

"Visit us at AFWERX and POOF! Innovative solutions will appear!"

AFWERX was going to be more understandable than unknowable neural complexities. Innovation was not secretive magic from the dark arts. Anyone could do it. Our members were fairly experienced researchers and practitioners of innovative approaches, so explaining our AFWERX approach should have been easy. Maybe it was, but we were so busy trying to get AFWERX started that it took us nearly a year to slow down, reflect and develop an understandable three-step process laying things out:

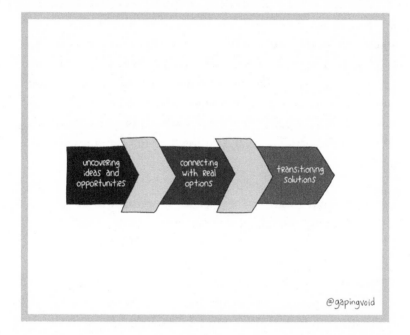

We could have created a five-step or seven-step process, but we followed Occam's razor that no explanation should be made more complex unless absolutely necessary. Our three stages seemed to cover our connecting and accelerating stages quite reasonably.

During stage one, we would listen and work with our "customers" to uncover or discover their problems, challenges, pain points or opportunities. "Opportunities" highlight how innovation could be useful outside of sheer necessity. Opportunities exist even when a process or system has been performing acceptably. For example, airmen can use chalkboards, slide rules and spreadsheets to create aircraft transportation travel schedules and fuel estimates. Even though the system is effective, it is not very efficient. There are often opportunities to improve processes like transportation scheduling dramatically by using optimization software.

Whether it is a problem or an opportunity, end-users of the product or service in question should be involved at every stage. Otherwise, you will miss out on key considerations. For example, during one of our earliest technology challenges, we were looking for different perimeter security solutions and counter-drone defense capabilities. As our team of 68 stakeholders from military, academic and industry backgrounds discussed the issues, a 20-something-year-old captain stood up and declared:

> "Look, I am a security force leader at one of our bases. We have to complete over 100 hours of training every year. I think it is great that so many people are interested in buying new technology for us, but please...please...if you are going to acquire something for your cops, please be sure that it reduces our training time in other areas. We simply do not have time in our overloaded schedules to learn another new technology system."

What was that? Training time? No one else in the room—not the strategists, not the researchers, not the technologists—had thought of that as a consideration. Training time might have been the most important consideration! If the innovations offered to security forces did not reduce training time in other activities, then the final technology solution would likely have been bought...and then placed upon a shelf somewhere to collect dust. Always, always, always have your end-users involved in your innovation actions.

During stage two, we worked with our customers to consider multiple solutions from industry, academia, existing government laboratories and other organizations. History has proven that competition among multiple efforts leads to greater innovation than single-solution sources. AFWERX avoided pre-defined solutions and "all eggs in one basket" approaches as we pursued prototyping agility (agility: options at the speed of relevance).

During stage three, a customer would take our prototype solution and consider whether they wanted to transition what we had created together into a permanent product or service for their organization. This required developing contracting pathways that allowed us to bridge from producing at a prototype level to producing at a larger scale.

BUILDING INNOVATION DEMAND AND SUPPLY

With our three-stage process established, we began to categorize our various AFWERX efforts on the basis of which stage they were most likely to support. In reality, AFWERX was a dynamic system with multi-directional connectivity flowing across numerous innovation efforts—we actually were a bit like a neural network! At the same time, and in our most user-friendly visual conception, AFWERX helped uncover our customers' innovation desires (demand) and matched them with innovation creation processes (supply) to help create new capabilities. The framework that emerged looked like this:

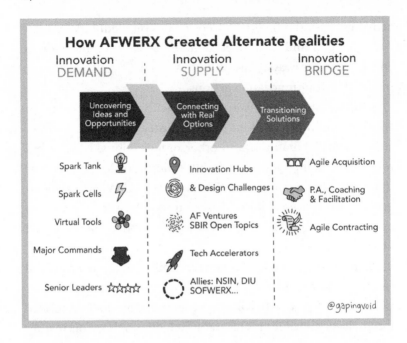

The supply and demand framework—or rather, innovation demand and supply framework—provided numerous communication benefits. Most importantly, it emphasized how innovation begins with Air Force customer demand—in other words, it was for the end-users. It also showed an intuitive progression of demand and supply matching, something that most people who have lived in capitalist economies understand. The visual was also brief and applicable. Lastly, it was also flexible, which was useful because when AFWERX started, we had five Capability areas. However, during our first 18 months, we grew to 12 Capability areas with Capability Leaders. The demand and supply system could accommodate our changing capabilities. The approach connected those with the *will* to innovate, whether they were part of the demand, supply or bridge of the system's flow.

A CLOSER LOOK

What follows is a brief overview of the various capabilities that AFWERX fused together to create its system of innovation demand and supply. But first...

BONUS GIFT!

If you visit the AFWERX website or type "AFWERX Book" into a search engine, you will find a link to the PDF file of *AFWERX: Empowering Next Generation Innovators and Innovations.*

The ebook will give you over 150 pages of deeper insight about AFWERX and our startup years' structure, as well as "Lessons Learned" and "Best Practices" of AFWERX's early years from multiple authors—our first wave of AFWERX Talent. I asked our Talent to write down their thoughts about our first two years, and they responded marvelously. If for some reason you cannot find the document on the web, send me an email (address in the closing chapter) and I will send it to you.

Since a "deep dive" of knowledge on AFWERX's structure and tactics is available for free on the internet, there is no need to repeat it here. Instead, what follows is a breezy description of the multiple ways AFWERX approached solving problems for our customers: the airmen. Some of these may be instantly replicable by your organization and some may simply be launching points for brainstorms about innovation capabilities you might tailor to your specific *Environment.*

PHASE 1: INNOVATION DEMAND

I. Spark Tank is an annual Air Force-wide competition that mirrors the format of the hit television show *Shark Tank.*

During Spark Tank, teams of airmen (and the occasional solo innovator) pitch their latest inventions to, and request funding from, our Air Force's most senior leaders, along with a few distinguished business leaders. This grand challenge event is open to all 680,000 airmen. Hundreds of entries are whittled down to six finalists during a six-month period. We were even fortunate enough to once have *Shark Tank* creator and entrepreneur Mark Cuban participate as a judge, further solidifying the *Shark Tank* comparison. This competition continues to grow in popularity—our 2020 Spark Tank received over 20,000 audience votes from digital devices! When possible, we also looked to support semifinalists' project ideas. Many generals and senior executives helped with the judging, and our partnership with the management division of the Pentagon was consistently fruitful for bringing this event together.

II. **Spark Cells** are Air Force Base innovation offices that provide airmen with tactical innovation capabilities that can be used at their base. The Spark Cells offer airmen connectivity with the broader innovation ecosystem, which allows airmen to solve the challenges that they experience while executing their missions. The Spark Cells are voluntary efforts—there is no designated "Base Level Innovator" career field within the Air Force. These innovators are volunteers who commit extra time to attend in-person and virtual training events. They also participate in "collider" events with businesses and academics to learn and sometimes fund experiments aimed at solving a base (or group of bases') challenges. The Spark Cell network grew to over 70 cells across the world in the first few years of AFWERX, from Japan to Alaska to Al Udeid.

III. **Virtual Tools** help bring together Air Force innovators from across the world. A collaborative, web-based platform allowed our airmen to work on ideas and advance projects from any base or their homes—anywhere, anytime! For example, the Spark Tank campaign of 2019-2020 was run on our virtual platform and included video submissions of approximately three minutes. Additionally, AFWERX was allowed to try an alternative system of office collaboration (Google G Suite, now Workspace) products which gave us the ability to collaborate on unclassified projects from our personal computers and mobile devices, as well as our government devices. This provided us greater agility and productivity by not needing to be anchored to government computers and government terminals. The Pentagon's Defense Digital Service granted us that waiver for our Google experiment—thank you, DDS!

IV. **Major Command (MAJCOM) Innovators** were a creative group of airmen whose efforts spanned multiple organizations with the goal of preventing different organizations from recreating the same wheel. To put it bluntly, these redundant "wheels" could have occurred as a result of the Air Force having specialized technology commands, such as a fighter aircraft command (Air Combat Command) and an airlift command (Air Mobility Command). The Air Force also has regional divisions such as the Pacific Air Forces Command and the US Air Forces in Europe Command. Much of each MAJCOM's attention is understandably inward-focused. Forming a combined cohort of MAJCOM Innovators allowed us to avoid separate, uncoordinated and redundant efforts and instead synergized our efforts to innovate for common interests. For example, all MAJCOMs benefit from satellite technologies for their intelligence and navigation needs; as a result, all MAJCOMs benefited from combining innovation efforts for areas such as better "persistent surveillance," "data encryption" and "electromagnetic pulse mitigation."

V. **Senior Leaders** provided support that made a difference. An organization can only rise to the level of its leaders, and during AFWERX's first three years, AFWERX benefited from the support of Vice Chief of Staff Gen Stephen Wilson, Lt Gen J.D. Harris, senior executive Jack Blackhurst and other senior leaders from organizations such as Plans and Programs, Financial Management, Acquisition and the Air Force Research Laboratory. Their investment included weekly meetings of advice and resourcing discussions during most of our first year, and monthly updates thereafter. As part of our relationship, we also worked to advance some of their areas of interest, including for Joint All-Domain Command and Control (JADC2) and Base of the Future innovation efforts.

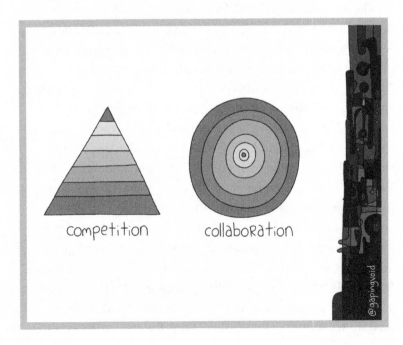

competition   collaboration

PHASE 2: SUPPLYING INNOVATION TO SATISFY DEMANDS

VI. **Innovation Hubs** are a unique contribution to any innovation program. On the one hand, they can be as simple as a one-person innovation office; on the other, for our 680,000-person organization of the Air Force, it was useful to have gathering places that were specifically designed to offer bigger gathering areas outside of bases with gate guards and fences. This saved a tremendous amount of time each year by not having to go through all of the security paperwork and clearances to allow people entry onto a base or a secured facility. Our hubs were also designed with more imagination than standard government grey cubicles and offered a friendlier welcome to new small business members and entrepreneurs.

A key question for any organization is: "How many hubs do we need?" Maybe you "need" zero, because there is already a great community space you can rent when the need arises, or there are facilitators whom you can hire. Alternatively, perhaps you would benefit from a minimally-staffed innovation hub with one full-time facilitator who could then seek out additional facilitators and support personnel for short-term surges of high activity.

If you do end up choosing to use more than one innovation hub, the next key consideration for you is whether you want those hubs to "compete" with or "complement" one another. Some organizations and budgets prefer similar hubs to be built in different locations to compete with one another to see who deserves more funding in future years. That approach was *not* the AFWERX way. We created three hubs and they were assigned distinctive but complementary roles.

Our AFWERX-DC hub offered a collaboration space of approximately 500 square feet for our AFWERX Pentagon personnel and collaborators, along with some common area space available on a "first-come, first-serve" basis. We resided in the Eastern Foundry office suite area of Crystal City, Virginia, and our nonprofit partner was Virginia Tech-Applied Research Corporation. VT-ARC helped us make informed, data-driven decisions through actionable data analysis and market research reports, as well as by identifying and connecting us with leading technology experts from industrial, academic and non-traditional sources.

AFWERX-Vegas was our gathering location for most facilitated innovation requests from Air Force organizations. The 20,000-square-foot facility within the Howard Hughes Center allowed multiple idea workshops, design sprints and proto-typing initiatives to occur simultaneously. It was created through a collaborative effort with DEFENSEWERX and evolved to have the facilitation capabilities being supplied by theDifference consulting group. Mark "Rocketeer" Rowland from ROCeteer Inc. was our AFWERX-Vegas leader during our startup years.

Las Vegas was chosen as the location for this hub due to an interesting formula I was taught while studying innovation at the SOFWERX innovation hub. Their guidance was that an innovation hub should be near a major airport and located in a city where there are interesting food, lodging and entertainment options for when visitors are not at the hub. Our AFWERX-Vegas location was within 15 minutes of the airport with more than a few hotel, food and entertainment options only a few blocks away on the Las Vegas Strip. Additionally, Las Vegas can average over a million visitors per week for innovative events such as CES (Consumer Electronics Show), DEFCON (hacking event), Interdrone (premier drone event) and AWS re:Invent. As a result, the city offered higher odds of collaborative serendipity. Lastly, our Vegas hub was near two prominent Air Force bases, just in case we needed end-users to offer their opinions on various projects.

AFWERX-Austin offered a unique way for airmen to interact with researchers and entrepreneurs and unleash the Air Force's innovative spirit. It was located within the innovation spaces of Austin's Capital Factory, a series of floors housing hundreds of software and hardware innovation businesses. AFWERX-Austin was run by Air Force reservists and guardsmen—the perfect fusion of military insight and business experience. They hosted workshops, facilitated some of our challenges, served on AFVentures teams (explained below) and also supported "collider" events that brought together Air Force innovation demanders and entrepreneurial suppliers.

VII. **Air Force Ventures** had a capability title with a dual meaning, which is appropriate given that it was based on dual-use technology (technology that can be used by both the government and the private sector). "Ventures" is a root word for "adventures," which AFWERX undertook with this innovation capability. At the same time, "ventures" was also slang for venture capital investments. The two meanings came together because a coalition of Air Force organizations was able to leverage a very interesting government allocation of money: Small Business Innovation Research (SBIR) funds. SBIR, pronounced "sibber," funds provide support for US small businesses to engage in Federal Research and Development with the hope of commercializing the end products.

The Department of Defense and 10 other government agencies have different approaches for creating SBIR grants and supporting America's small business innovation capabilities. For example, one government agency might announce that it was looking for a widget, and then describe the 40 or more characteristics that the widget should possess. This kind of specificity greatly reduces the number of small businesses that will respond and participate, because most small businesses will not be able to meet all of the stated requirements.

AFWERX and our *Coalition of the Willing* partners—The SBIR Center of Excellence at Wright-Patterson Air Force Base and the Air Force Acquisition Ventures division of the Pentagon —took a different approach. Instead of approaching businesses with precise technical specs to which a widget should conform, we worked with our partner organizations to form an "Open Topic." The Open Topic approach was similar to shouting to small businesses "Hey! What are you creating that you think would be useful for the Air Force?" This question approach tremendously increased the number of responses to SBIR requests, as well as the number of options from which Air Force demanders could choose. Previous to the AFWERX experiment, the highest response rate to traditional Air Force SBIR solicitations was a little less than 70 proposals. With the SBIR Open Topic approach, our coalition received over 1,000 proposals multiple times during our "Open Topic" queries.

Given that one of AFWERX's "Drive Innovation...to secure our future" initiatives was to expand our network of defense business partners, the thousands of proposals and over 700 new companies subsequently contracted and supporting our Nation's defense were notable achievements for our *Mission*.

When AFWERX started in 2017, AFVentures was not even a concept. However, our open environment for ideas and experimentation allowed our Talent to apply their creative skill to form new capabilities, apply their *will* and achieve results.

VIII. **Tech Accelerators** were an experimental capability that ran its course (for AFWERX, anyway). Part of the reason for briefly discussing the Tech Accelerator capability is the fact that we ended it after three rounds of yearly experiments.

The Tech Accelerator was a program designed to allow us

to talk to 10 companies while they were still in their startup phase. The two-way discussions allowed us to influence the way that the products were developed, because the companies would take our suggestions as demand signals of what would make their products more attractive for government purchase. Our business partner for this process was the highly effective TechStars.

The companies participating in our accelerator process had the unique feature of all working on "dual-use" technologies that would be of interest to both the US government and the commercial sector. For example, in 2019, there was a drone capture system that used mini-missiles to launch strips of latex confetti at unwelcomed drones and gum up the drones' propellers, leading to their capture. This approach was seen as safer than exploding a drone, which may be carrying chemicals. This capture system could be useful for both our government (e.g., military base defense) as well as civilian organizations, such as airports (London's Heathrow comes to mind).

In the end, our efforts with the Tech Accelerator inspired other organizations in the Air Force to form their own Tech Accelerator programs, so we no longer felt AFWERX had to champion this experiment. Additionally, we determined that our Ventures experiment would be able to produce a greater magnitude of prototypes for our Air Force, and so we shifted our Talent and funding to that effort. This resourcing shift reflected our "experimental" culture. AFWERX would attempt multiple innovation "experiments" and continue with the ones that offered the most value. Value was not based on quantity metrics alone. For example, our Spark Tank "only" produced six finalists, but it generated hundreds of ideas from airmen and boundless amounts of innovative culture across our Air Force.

. . .

IX. **Allies** come in all forms and sizes, from a single connecting person or expert to an entire organization. No one travels the innovation road alone, and allies were integral to AFWERX's success. Since AFWERX began with fewer than a dozen people, if we were going to help an organization of 680,000 become more innovative and agile, we would need to join with value-adding partners.

Allies helped us pursue a common set of interests through voluntary contributions of resources. For example, SOFWERX hosted me so I could learn at their hub for a month in 2017, and they later joined us for a counter-drone challenge in 2018. Additionally, the National Security Innovation Network (NSIN) helped us link some of our Air Force offices to university innovation teams through their "Hacking for Defense" program.

We also had allies in the Air Force. For example, the Air Force Research Laboratory offered us a lot of connectivity and capability from people donating their time and expertise. The Pentagon's Air Force Management division helped build the virtual collaboration system that would host virtual innovation efforts such as Spark Tank inputs. There are many more examples, but for now, these few anecdotes highlight that allies magnified our *will* and its collective effects.

PHASE 3: THE BRIDGE OF TRANSITION

The "Valley of Death" could be the name of a first-person shooter video game or the seemingly impossible task of transitioning a prototype into a full-scale capability program for the Air Force. To help airmen and Air Force organizations traverse the Valley of Death, we cultivated three capabilities that did not exist at AFWERX when we first started. They were:

X. **Agile Acquisition** was not AFWERX's most publicly visible tool. Even so, it was one of the most effective. The Federal Acquisition Regulation (FAR) is thousands of pages thick, so having a wise acquisition specialist—and allies who also understood acquisition options—was immensely helpful. They helped Air Force organizations develop pathways that allowed our airmen to purchase prototypes and prep them for larger quantity purchases. Our acquisition specialists also tracked congressional rule changes and found FAR and non-FAR options for prototyping and purchasing solutions.

XI. **Public Affairs, Coaching and Facilitation** capabilities helped answer the question: "If an innovation falls in the woods and no one hears about it, does it make a sound?" Public Affairs and Marketing offered many ways for us to advance our innovation mission externally. At the same time, we advanced innovation projects internally by teaming airmen with coaches and facilitators. I will defer to *AFWERX: Empowering Next Generation Innovators and Innovations* reading for deeper discussion here, but I would like to offer one strong recommendation: you need a website. Period. It can be simple but looking non-governmental grey is probably a good idea. It should have a calendar, a way for people to sign up to receive a monthly newsletter of events, a way for people to offer their technologies and a link highlighting how the empowered Talent of your organizations created successes. You should (when you have enough people) offer interesting content, and when possible, expand to social media posting. For your consideration, please visit the AFWERX website at https://afwerx.af.mil.

XII. **Agile Contracting** may also not seem too exciting compared to prototyping triumphs and defeats, but you need that calm, wise professional who knows how to set up a contract between the government and a business or nonprofit organization. There are so many rules and considerations with spending government dollars. AFWERX did not begin with its own contracting capability, but over time we found reliable, expert help that was much appreciated.

· · ·

This chapter began by noting something interesting: organizations are creating value without needing to have physical objects to offer—their value came from what they connected. AFWERX was structured in a similar way. We built a virtual and in-person platform that connected innovation demands with innovation suppliers and then offered a bridge to help our warfighters cross over the Valley of Death in order to purchase their prototypes and help prepare Air Force organizations for larger purchases. AFWERX was not simply an innovation mission; we were an innovation <u>empowerment</u> mission.

INCREASING POSITIVE FLOW WITHIN STRUCTURE

*How would you describe your current or anticipated innovation structure? Do you have your own prototyping capabilities? Are you a "connector platform" or something else? Are you willing to allow your structure to evolve?

*How much competition, variety and "broad portfolio" of small option efforts are you pursuing? How are you avoiding an "all eggs in one basket" structure? Are multiple clients providing innovation demands? Are you supplying—or connecting—multiple innovation capabilities to solve challenges?

*Is your innovation effort a supply capability, demand capability or both? How are you connecting that system with other suppliers or demanders? Are you linked with contracting officials, acquisition officials and other legal experts to help your prototypes transition into larger scales of quantities?

*Do you want to own all portions of your Demand, Supply and Bridging, or are there already reliable allies within your *Environment*?

*How might you virtually collaborate and provide opportunities "anywhere and anytime" for a person who would like to innovate?

*Are there somewhat isolated or stove-piped divisions in your organization (e.g., regional or technological distinct groupings) that could send representatives (part-time or full-time) to join a diverse, cross-organization innovation team?

*How many innovation hubs or gathering spaces do you need? With what kind of full-time and part-time structure? Do you want your hubs to compete with one another or specialize with complementary skills? By what criteria are you choosing your hub locations and staffing (i.e., skills, connectivity to other skills)?

6

INPUTS AND PROCESSES:
TWO SECRET INGREDIENTS

I was nearly 46 years old before I finally discovered "the recipe" for slow-baked, soft-batch chocolate chip cookies. For hundreds of Sundays since, my kiddos and I have baked 18

cookies at a time, tinkering with everything from the brand of butter to the brand of baking sheets, and you better believe those cookie sheets are designated "for cookie baking only." Twenty-one minutes in our oven (not 20), rotating the cookie sheets in the oven midway through the baking process and using two cups of chocolate chips versus the recommended one cup are just a few of our subtle modifications that add up to a memorable cookie experience. I will not claim my cookies are the best of all time, but I will submit that many eaters of these bigger-than-your-palm cookies have taken their first bite and said, "Now that's a good cookie."

Such quality is not an accident. As I admitted, it was the result of over two years of tinkering with an already good recipe and changing baking *Inputs and Processes* until it became a dependable set of actions that yielded high quality every time. The recipe is still simple and does not look that different from an average recipe, but two general components—the quality of *Inputs* and the nuances within the *Processes*—add up to a better result.

There were two critical components to our AFWERX development that we leveraged again and again during our startup years to rise to world-class innovation status. They were:

1. Build upon our strengths as *Inputs* for our actions
2. Use an innovation *Process* that included vetting for five key ingredients

Although those two *Inputs and Processes* look simple enough, they are part of thousands of tweaks across the decades within the recipes of innovative thinking. A seemingly endless stream of books, courses and entire degrees have been dedicated to design and innovation. For my own recipe development, I would like to thank our Talented Airmen, Allies, and the "chefs" at Michigan State (leadership and change management MBA, political science BA), Penn State (appreciative inquiry and organization development courses), RAND Graduate School (policy analysis PhD) and the University of Virginia (design thinking courses). The insights offered by those experiences directly affected the recipe of AFWERX's development.

Additionally, if I were to make a Top Five list of action-oriented books that guided my contribution to the AFWERX mission, I would probably pick:

The Four Steps to the Epiphany by Steve Blank
Leading Change by John Kotter
The Unnatural Act of Management by Everett T. Suters
The Seven Habits of Highly Effective People by Stephen Covey
Reinventing Organizations by Frederic Laloux

Lastly, another giant upon whose shoulders I stood was Abraham Maslow. Maslow developed a Hierarchy of Needs model that, at its summit, shows people being most fulfilled when they achieve self-actualization. I tried to bring self-actualization to the AFWERX organization by giving as much liberty as possible to our talented members, so that they could self-actualize by (my blunt definition follows) using their strengths in meaningful ways to achieve a fulfilling purpose. Building from strengths was a key ingredient in the AFWERX recipe during our startup years, and it included deliberate team reflection on our individual and organizational traits (including by using various personality tests).

The remainder of this chapter elaborates upon those two key components of *Inputs* and *Processes*, beginning with the leveraging of our people and our organization's strengths.

THE SEARCH
FOR MEANING
BEGINS WITH

THE SEARCH
FOR PURPOSE

@gapingvoid

STRENGTHS INSIGHT #1: POSITIVE, FLUID FOCUS

Even a reliably good recipe can be spoiled by low-quality ingredients. For this reason, you want to have worthy objectives as the starting basis for your actions. Worthy objectives can generate motivation and the *will* to perform, even when team members are otherwise physically tired. A worthy purpose is positively focused, highlighting what you want to do (versus what you want to avoid).

As I have written previously, words matter, and a simple contrast can illustrate that point. Imagine how you might feel if you were part of a "problem-solving team" for an airline and were given the following objective:

The purpose of our gathering is to root out the causes of why our luggage is experiencing a four percent "lost or late" rating.

Alternatively, imagine how you might feel if you were part of an "organizational advancement team" for an airline given the following objective:

The purpose of our gathering is to uncover what creates an excellent customer luggage experience for our customers who entrust us with their valuables.

Each wording of the two objectives has the potential to reduce the amount of lost or late luggage, yet one approach will be more likely to lead to blame, negativity and finger-pointing. In contrast, the other approach highlights people at their finest and offers a chance for them to be appreciated. We build our evaluation lenses and reactions with our word choices. As we choose our words, we simultaneously construct and anticipate future realities, choosing to build upon our strengths with professional, poetic and positive words. Alternatively, people can decide to focus on negative weaknesses and spiral their gatherings emotionally downward.

Word choice also matters at the individual level. Simple, subtle messages send signals. For example, consider a two-person communication meeting. Whether a boss is speaking to a subordinate, a parent to a child or a romantic partner to another, suppose that one person says to another, "Don't forget to...(insert action)." That kind of negative wording focuses on the other person's weakness, citing that they are capable of forgetting and that they should avoid being their defective self. That kind of messaging is not particularly uplifting for the *will*. By contrast, a message such as "Please remember to...(insert action)" speaks to the better part of a person's capabilities.

The positive, poetic and strategic framing of words can be used at all levels, whether personal or organizational. As a team member or a team leader, using a positive focus gives your objectives and your organization a more uplifting purpose.

Word choice can also matter with regard to your scope of possible impacts. For example, imagine an "old school" trainer at a fitness gym who believes that the only way to accomplish a great workout is to have trainers standing next to their clients as they accomplish their routines. When COVID-19 spread into the United States and virus mitigation policies prevented gatherings at public gyms, some of those trainers had to shut down their business. "If I cannot meet with my client in person, then I have no impact," was uttered by more than a few personal trainers.

However, other trainers (and organizations) began offering "virtual" training and coaching with home gym equipment. Their more open mindset allowed them to maintain contact with their clients, even if at a reduced price. Additionally, a virtual approach allowed trainers to take on even more clients by eliminating the drive time to different homes and fitness centers, and by cutting downtime spent waiting for late clients. Paid time slots are paid time slots, and much of the *Environment's* randomness from travel and gathering was reduced. The COVID-19 restrictions allowed some innovative people to try new ways of connecting with clients, which will likely shape the way fitness training is conducted in the future. Innovative people, when given lemons, look for ways to make lemonade. Innovative people also look for very fluid words when describing who they are and what they do.

During AFWERX's startup years, we were very conscientious about word choices that would allow our efforts a flexible scope. Let us look at our mission as a self-description:

AFWERX: A fusion of capabilities <u>who</u> connects innovators and accelerate results to create Air Force cultural and technological agility.

We avoided popular descriptions such as "team of teams,"

because sometimes our Capability Leaders were solo "teams of one." We also avoided "system of systems" because the <u>who</u> and *we* of our full-time and part-time Talent were the keys to our success. We found flexible fluidity in the phrase "fusion of capabilities." Whether we were discussing our virtual or in-person capabilities or our demand, supply and bridge capabilities, the "fusion" description provided us the flexibility to grow, shrink or rearrange our innovation resources as we saw fit. Words matter.

KEEP THE MAGIC. DO THE WORK.

@gapingvoid

STRENGTHS INSIGHT #2: BUILD FROM A CREDIBLE HISTORY

Have you ever experienced a hollow impact from an attempted motivational speech? For example, have you heard a speech that had nothing but generic phrases such as "we are going to take it to the next level" or "our destiny awaits" or "you should be excited to be a part of this?" When these types of speeches end, you may feel no more motivated than you were at the beginning, and you may even be a bit irritated because you lost productive time listening to a hollow speech.

Rather than relying upon hollow speeches from one "mastermind" speaker in an authority position, using individual strengths from all the people in your organization provides a credible way for everyone to become engaged and motivated about where the organization is "positively" headed. As with word choice, the credible history nuance adds to the quality of your innovation recipe.

Whether at an individual or organizational level, when people are asked to "think back to a time of strength," it can lead to discomfort. People may not like to talk about themselves if they think it sounds like bragging. One way to help people feel more comfortable with a strengths exploration is to offer the following thought experiment from professional basketball:

Imagine that you are the coach of a professional basketball team, and that your team's hard work and grit have resulted in reaching the NBA Finals. Congratulations to you!

Now, it is two days before the championship series opener and you are considering how to spend your time preparing for the game. Which approach do you think will be more effective?

a. You will build a strategy around the star players guiding your team. Maybe you have a Michael Jordan or a LeBron James on your team, or maybe you have a one-two punch like a Kobe Bryant and Shaquille O'Neal.

b. You will improve upon a technique that is weakest in your team, such as the overall three-point shooting average (due to the poor percentage by your ninth- and 10th-best players on the team). Your star players' roles will receive no unique attention as you prepare for the championship.

Given the choice between the star players guiding the whole team or reducing the weaknesses of individual components, most of us who are familiar with sports and the psychology of coaches and players would likely make the same choice—when the game is on the line, you will tend to use your strengths. Even if the "reduce weaknesses" approach improves the team's three-point shooting average by improving the ninth- and 10th-best players' accuracy, those players are still likely to be sitting on the bench during game time. When it is game time, you as the coach are probably not going to pursue a new grand strategy of three-point shooting with your ninth- and 10th-best players at the expense of your LeBrons and Kobes. You will most likely play to your strengths.

AFWERX played to our players' strengths in various ways, including by reviewing a credible history of our strengths to bring forth the stories that uncovered our positive *will.* You and your organization can do this, too. This kind of activity helps remind your Talent that they possess true, credible strengths that your organization can develop as it constructs an alternate reality for the future. A strength is something that energizes you even as you exert effort while attempting to create meaningful results. In other words, you will not have to depend on magic to get there, and you can avoid hollow speeches from some authority figure.

At the same time, reviewing strengths also helps combat a common weakness people have: their belief that if they can do it, anyone can. The bias we have towards "anyone can do this" is simply not true. If you have the ability to read a 50-page, data-filled report and create a single slide summary of it in a way that can accurately inform decisions, that is a strength. If you can build wooden picture frames easily because you have tinkered with wood carving tools your whole life, that is a strength. The list of strengths within your organization is probably large, and a strengths-based review will help you uncover some of the most relevant ones.

In the summer of 2020, we at AFWERX had just been ranked #16 in the world as a *Best Workplace for Innovators* by Fast Company, which had evaluated 865 organizations. We wanted to capture what we felt had made our mission successful, and so we completed the following questions during our Common Mind gathering:

Scenario: Think back to two experiences (AFWERX or non-AFWERX related) that were exceptional, with you at your best —productive and effective while also enjoying the effort and being energized by it.

Describe those with:
a. A newspaper or website-style headline that is seven words or less
b. Up to two behaviors/actions exhibited during the experience, by you or other participants
c. Optional: any feelings or unique circumstances associated with the event

1a. Headline:
1b. Positively framed behaviors and actions
i.
ii.
1c. Optional:

2a. Headline:
2b. Positively framed behaviors and actions
i.
ii.
2c. Optional

The format for the exercise is not a rigid structure. For our AFWERX journey, I chose the format of a seven-words-or-less headline to help focus our Talent's words into the most important impact of the event or experience. The headlines can be, and often are, emotive and attention-grabbing, just like peak experiences. With the emotional part of the experience in mind, the person doing this exercise can then focus on the positive actions and behaviors that they remember connected to the event. The third, optional part was one more chance to note emotions, unusual circumstances or factors that may also have played a role.

For this strengths reflection, we broke up our 30 or so virtual Common Mind attendees into six groups, each with a facilitator who had reviewed the exercise with me the day prior. The facilitator for each group then worked within their groups to determine the top three behaviors and actions from everyone's responses. The group answers were then briefed to all Common Mind attendees. As we merged and analyzed our answers, we found great commonality in seven themes of strength that could be categorized in two broad areas: our *Mission* and our *Talent*. More specifically, AFWERX had:

Unique Gravity, Attractive Mission
-Purpose-driven mission and forward vision results in Fulfillment, Happiness and Satisfaction
-Willingness to creatively "experiment" and adapt with anything...even against the odds
-Objective and principled approach to solving Warfighter problems

Humble, World Class, Empowered Talent
-Play beyond our strengths when empowered and trusted with autonomy
-Positive perseverance, resiliency and grit

-Honest, transparent teamwork and collaboration that builds trusted relationships
-Talent training that results in Fulfillment, Happiness and Satisfaction

These insights are mostly self-explanatory, so further elaboration will not be necessary here—but it was really fulfilling to observe so many common strength *Inputs* within our "Common Mind."

STRENGTHS INSIGHT #3: ENVISION THE IDEAL

The previous "cogs" graphic from Gapingvoid (thank you, GV!) speaks to the opposite of a humble strengths journey. Sometimes an unexpected graphic or message helps further generate culture conversations. Demonizing undesired behaviors in a non-threatening, almost comical way can help remind people "we do not want to be like that."

In thinking about what we at AFWERX *did* want to be like, the natural next step after examining past strengths was to consider the future. During that same 2020 Common Mind gathering, we used the following individual format:

Scenario: Two years from now, as you wake up, you look around and see that AFWERX is what you always wished and dreamed AFWERX would be. Describe what AFWERX is known for and two actions—whether adjustments or continuations—that will make this reality occur.

Describe those with:
a. A newspaper or website style headline that is seven words or less
b. Up to two behaviors/actions exhibited during the experience, by you or other participants
c. Optional: any feelings or other unique circumstances associated with the event

1a. Headline:
1b. Positively framed behaviors and actions
i.
ii.
1c. Optional:

2a. Headline:
2b. Positively framed behaviors and actions
i.
ii.
2c. Optional

As before, we then merged and analyzed our top three

group answers and found many commonalities. This time, our ideal thoughts could be segmented into eight broad themes:

When AFWERX...
-Properly scales for agility
-Transparently communicates roles and ops tempo calendar plans based in humility
-Constantly, deliberately, evolves and learns with the unknown...and the bureaucracy
-Streamlines known processes and pathways
-Consistently recruits and invests in Talent
-Objectively engages in data-driven best practices and principled experimentation

Then AFWERX...
-Will have its culture embraced by our Air Force—experimentation and learning for anyone
-Will be desired worldwide as an uplifting innovation leader and desired partner for business, government and academia

Once again, most of these insights are self-explanatory and covered throughout this book. Even so, we might benefit by considering a bit more deeply why the reflections on Talent development and recruitment were so important for AFWERX.

talent's skill level

		low	high
leader's trust of talent	low	coaching	micromanagement
	high	naïve negligence	empowerment

@gapingvoid

There was a certain *FLOW* to the way all of the factors affecting AFWERX's *will* fit together. For example, our empowerment approach would not be an automatic solution for other innovation missions. There are preconditions to empowerment —namely, that you need a properly skilled team before you can say, "Okay, you are in charge of this capability—off you go!"

If your Talent is not properly trained for the tasks at hand, then to simply empower them and walk away is a form of neglect that will probably lead to negative consequences for their morale and *will*, as well as for your efforts. Similarly, when a new member joins your mission team, you will likely spend more time familiarizing them with your organization, the new member's assigned duties and how the new member contributes to the mission. During AFWERX's startup years, nearly all of our government members took the same design thinking courses from the Darden School of Business. This helped ensure that we had a common baseline for discussing innovation concepts and processes; it also increased our trust that others would make productive use of their empowered autonomy within our *W.A.T.E.R.* culture.

We saw some extreme contrasts to empowered decision-making from some other organizations during our startup years. We encountered some missions where the people seemed overly empowered without agreed-upon goals, OKRs or even shared oversight. Lacking a focusing, central intent, their collective *will* was rather scattered and not very effective. At the other extreme, we encountered organizations where no meaningful decisions could be made unless a general or senior executive civilian approved them. Senior leaders are busy people, and having to wait until a senior leader is available to say "Yes" is not a particularly agile strategy. A properly scoped, small-bet innovation project should not require an executive's approval.

Proper training was a crucial but not-easily-seen ingredient that helped our Talent accomplish their mission, because they felt empowered and skilled at handling their tasks. As a result, we could be more agile and productive during our startup years because our frontline innovators did not need to wait for permission from some expert authority figure. Our frontline innovators *were* the trusted experts.

STRENGTHS INSIGHT #4: BUILD A BRIDGE TO THE FUTURE AND TRAVEL IT

The remaining steps of a strengths-based journey can be summarized with the question: "Given our current status, what steps can we take in the next three months, six months or year to move closer to our ideal?" The choice of time frame is dependent upon the situation. For example, if you perform a strengths-based review of yourself, you may find behaviors you want to adopt immediately. For organizations, the time frame for action steps will likely be longer due to various stakehold-ers' schedules needing to be synchronized, resources needing to be shifted and other bureaucratic reasons.

Whatever the scope or scale of your strengths-based review, some version of a SMART goal—Specific, Measurable, Attain-able, Relevant and Time-based—should probably be framing your chosen steps and activities. You or your organization do not have to achieve a perfect vision during these calendar plan-ning sessions, but your specificity of pursuits and *will* should emerge stronger as a result.

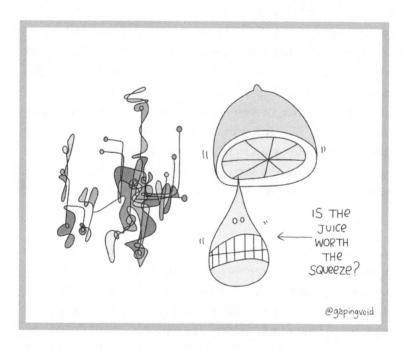

SECRET COMPONENT #2: EVALUATE FIVE KEY GOVERN-MENT INNOVATION INGREDIENTS

The strengths-based approach could be used for almost any challenging situation, whether it is improving your organiza-tion or brainstorming future ideas. By contrast, the five key ingredients are a bit more specific for government innovation projects. They help you evaluate the difference between a good innovation idea ready for experimental development and an idea that may need a little more work before you invest people, money or time. When AFWERX was approached with innovation ideas, our *Process* began with assessing whether the project (or "experiment") had the minimum factors necessary to start the journey towards success. Those five key ingredients were:

I: Intrapreneur: Who will be the project's champion? AFWERX could do much to provide innovative answers to challenging problems, but unless there was a project champion(s) who was willing to persist in solving a problem, including all of the little extra steps it might take to achieve an approval, that project stood little chance of being carried through to a successful conclusion. AFWERX successfully connected and collaborated with intrapreneurs who were end-users of innovative ideas, as well as non-end-users such as acquisition program managers (who then invited end-users to key meetings).

II. Resourced Advocates: Plenty of good innovation ideas are proposed every day. One way of prioritizing them is to ask the person proposing the idea: "Have you secured any funding for your idea?" This pragmatic question helps reveal ideas that other people found valuable by someone other than the person proposing it. After all, the bringer of the idea may have a bias in their idea valuation. Funding also provides a confidence signal that the proposed "experiment" has a reasonable chance of leading to a productive result. AFWERX did not have much of an investment fund for interesting projects, and even when we did, we preferred to offer "matching funds" to a project leader who had already obtained funding (through some form of project review). We had to use some kind of selection criteria for picking the projects that we would pursue with intrapreneurs, and "financial resources secured" was one such criterion. It was not the only one, but it was common to most.

III. Solution Providers: Whether through competition or commercial off-the-shelf products and services, a solution to an intrapreneur's challenge often resides within a technology. Connecting innovators to these option suppliers—government laboratories, industry, academia, entrepreneurs—was a key factor for obtaining innovation solutions. Within government innovation, a solution provider typically had to satisfy some kind of competitively priced review or unique capability justification through some kind of government market research. This is a major government purchasing constraint. Non-government entities have much greater flexibility and speed when choosing which tech products they would like to buy.

IV. Engaged Leadership: An organization, mission or singular project can only rise to the level of its leader's vision and support. If intrapreneurs have leaders who support their innovation efforts, then good *will* can be created. However, if a leader opposes an innovation effort or is apathetically neutral towards innovation efforts, then the efforts will likely collapse. Some level of leadership support, such as a memo, an email or even a public verbal acknowledgment of support to pursue a project for a few hours per week, appeared useful for airmen guiding their projects to success.

V. Enabling Capabilities—Public Affairs (Marketing and Communication), Contracting and Legal: "Early and often thereafter."

That phrase captures how frequently innovators should engage with these three critical allies. You are far more likely to reach a "Yes, if..." path for new experiments if you gain the brainstorming and project shaping insights from the teammates possessing these core skills. A "Yes, if..." mentality should also be accompanied by an appropriate sense of urgency—for AFWERX, this was a powerful lesson learned. Many government innovation projects end up being reviewed by a consensus-based team, which means that discomfort or unfamiliarity by any member can bring a project to a screeching halt. The answer? Overcommunicate, overcommunicate, overcommunicate. AFWERX did not have full-time allies in these enabling capability areas during our beginnings, and we were not as effective as we could have been as a result.

There was no cookie-cutter recipe for all AFWERX innovation efforts and our structure contained many different capabilities. However, there were definite commonalities in our actions. Our *Inputs* of talented people, time and funding were strengths we built upon, and our *Processes* were prioritized based upon five key ingredients. Together, they helped create an innovation recipe with strong chances for success. There are no guarantees with innovation efforts, but there are ways to stack the odds in your favor.

Within our *FLOW* model, we have now seen how AFWERX was created in response to the need for greater innovation in our *Environment*, and we successfully built our world-class capability by pursuing our *Mission and Strategy* with a *Culture* that allowed for an agile *Structure* with a variety of *Inputs and Processes* built upon the strengths of our talented people and their capabilities.

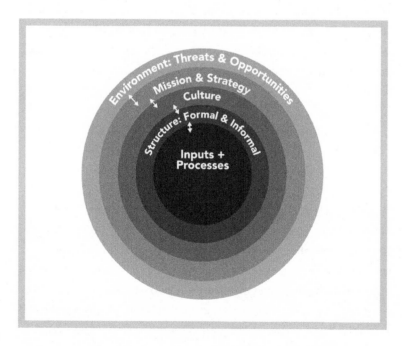

INCREASING POSITIVE FLOW WITH INPUTS AND PROCESSES

*How does your organization focus efforts for positive action at the individual and organizational levels? How are words and focus selected for gatherings, emails, newsletters and other communiques?

*Have you recently uncovered a credible history of strengths with yourself, your people and your organization? For your consideration, the methods offered in this chapter were effective for AFWERX and could probably be adopted for use with your team (we accomplished most of our answering within approximately four hours of virtual work).

* Have you recently uncovered an ideal future based upon the strengths within yourself, your people and your organization? What does your ideal future look like? Within what timeline? Is additional training required for some or all of your members? What kind of training would advance your organization toward an ideal future while also motivating and empowering your team?

*How are your project champions end-user-focused?
*What criteria of "ingredients" would you use for prioritizing project efforts?

*Can your meeting structure and level of leader interaction adapt to your level of familiarity and trust? For example, if you have new members on your team, then you may need more meetings or training until the team is pretty comfortable and familiar with what each other is doing. After some time, are you ready to shed some meetings that may no longer be as valuable to your more experienced members?

7

OUTPUT AND FEEDBACK:
EXTERNAL, INTERNAL AND NATURAL

@gapingvoid

Topics such as *Output and Feedback* can initially look rather dry and boring...until you place them within the *Environments* of an *American Idol* or *America's Got Talent* audition. For years, millions of people have tuned in to these reality shows to watch the audition episodes. Viewers are amazed and amused by the unskilled contestants who believe that their *Output* of an entertainment routine is mind-blowingly good. However, when the unpolished performers receive *Feedback* from the judges that their *Output* should be covered with cat litter, it is the participants who have their minds blown and dreams dashed.

Most of us have had numerous experiences with *Output* and *Feedback,* and entire courses of study have been developed to cover all the nuances and tradeoffs of various surveys and assessments. "Yeah, but..." can be applied to almost any method of evaluation because no single tool can make a leader or organization omniscient. Still, some well-designed feedback is typically useful (if imperfect), so this chapter will focus on a few key considerations that benefited AFWERX and that should benefit other innovation organizations as well.

ROI: EFFICIENCY, EFFECTIVENESS OR COST-SAVINGS WHEN POSSIBLE

The following *Feedback* facts from this story are not as important as how the story demonstrates ways of messaging an innovation *Output* as a return on investment (ROI):

Over a seven-year period, the Air Force tried to build a new helmet for its pilots. Two different efforts were attempted. The combined efforts cost approximately $7 million and yielded only one usable prototype that no one wanted to purchase for use throughout the Air Force. Helmets can be tricky to create—trying to integrate communications equipment while keeping the product lightweight, comfortable and able to withstand the stress of high-pressure environments that apply many times the force of gravity are all significant engineering challenges.

AFWERX was approached by an Air Force office for collaborative help in creating new helmet prototypes. This collaborative effort produced a very different, positive outcome. Taking a crowdsourced approach to acquiring technical solutions yielded 37 different potential possibilities for helmet creation. From this gathering of options, three approaches were selected for competitive testing. The collaborative effort cost approximately $1 million.

To recap: the Air Force spent seven years and $7 million to end with no desired prototypes whereas AFWERX's collaborative method of approximately seven months and $1 million resulted in three highly desired prototypes. The final helmet selection is scheduled for 2021.

The previous story highlights an important part about innovative *Output*: you will benefit from providing *Feedback* that shows the "value add" from your innovation efforts. Resources of people, money and time have been dedicated to make your innovation happen—so what? What was the impact?

In the private sector, improvements to a product or a process can usually be linked to greater sales and greater profits. Profits are not typically an option within the government *Environment*. As a result, we need to be providing *Feedback* to our stakeholder groups about how their investment is providing a "net benefit" to them. Not every innovation can be easily communicated with an equivalent dollar value, but whenever possible, you should communicate examples demonstrating more efficient outcomes (same effect with less effort), more effective outcomes (better effect per effort) or cost-reducing outcomes.

In collaboration with intrapreneurs, AFWERX produced impacts during its startup years that told the tale about dollar and personnel ROI, including:

Effectiveness: Improving AI data operations.

Efficiency: Robotic process automation "bots" that performed mundane digital paperwork forms faster and more reliably than humans.

Cost Reductions: Creating equipment with better ergonomics which reduced future personnel medical injuries and costs.

More specific details about individual AFWERX projects can be found in the AFWERX ebook at www.afwerx.af.mil. The goal of this chapter is to provide general insights into the *FLOW* factors of *Output* and *Feedback*. If you cannot articulate a "bottom line" impact, then you may soon no longer have a bottom line to worry about.

	individual	group
external	E l	EG
internal	l l	lG

@gapingvoid

FOUR FEEDBACK FORUMS: "US" AND "THEM"

Feedback, and communication more generally, may be broadly categorized into the four areas shown in the figure above. Whether individually or as a group, your organization benefits from considering the thoughts of external stakeholders, and the same applies to your internal communications. We should not lose sleep pondering the distinctions between "internal" and "external" too much, because some individuals, such as a resource provider, could be placed into either category.

By contrast, the individual and group distinctions are worth investigating a bit more. The moment you switch from interviewing one person at a time to interviewing people together, the *Feedback* will likely change. For example, focus groups and small group interviews can cause people to reduce their extreme comments and water down their preferences to conform with a group's general direction—not always, but there are multiple possible biases from group interactions that are well documented.

At the same time, group discussions can stimulate a greater number of total unique ideas than if the same individuals were asked to generate ideas by themselves and then have them tallied together. When you look to obtain *Feedback* on your *Output*, you should consider the inherent strengths and weaknesses that your data collection approaches will contain. A few key observations from our startup years follow, and guess what? Once again, a diversified approach for feedback was preferred and yielded useful insights.

EXTERNAL FEEDBACK: INDIVIDUALS AND GROUPS

During design thinking coursework, we encountered a saying:

"I would rather have 10 people answer 100 questions than 100 people answer 10 questions."

The meaning of this saying is that the depth and nuance you can learn from individual interviews can be substantial. To illustrate, you may recall the example from Chapter 5 about the value of the insight from an individual security officer thinking out loud about different perimeter security solutions and counter-drone defense capabilities. Although our team of 68 stakeholders from military, academic and industrial back-grounds discussed countless issues, it took one 20-something-year-old captain to stop us in our tracks: whatever solution we came up with needed to account for reducing the training hours to security forces' already-overloaded schedules.

No one else in the room had thought of training time as a consideration, and it might have been the most important one! This kind of insight would <u>not</u> have been uncovered if we had only used a number scale survey to evaluate different tech-nology options. Questions such as: "On a scale of 1 to 5, how effective do you think this solution will be?" would have missed the important nuance of training-time impacts. As an addi-tional consideration, survey response rates can be low. It is not unusual to see less than 33 percent of any group responding to a survey.

Another example of valuable individual insight occurred during our 2019 AFWERX Fusion event. I was walking through the innovative companies' showcase area and I stopped to talk with an innovator at his display area.

"What do you think of our AFWERX event?" I asked the entrepreneur. "You can be completely honest. We are still young, and there is still a lot of tolerance for mistakes. You cannot hurt my feelings."

"Honestly, Beam," began the gentleman, "this has been a great gathering."

"Well, thanks for that, we do try hard," I began, "but what happens if you are not selected as a finalist? You gave up days of travel and time here when you could have been working more on your business."

He smiled, pointed to a back corner of his table and replied, "Look over there, Beam. Do you see that pile of business cards?"

I nodded.

"There must be at least 25 cards there. They represent opportunities to work with other businesses gathered here and build a combined product. Do you know how tough it can be to find a credible, compatible business partner? There is *no way* we would have found 25 other companies this week, or even in a few weeks, like we found at this event. Even if we do not get a contract from this event, the connections we have made have been more than worth the investment."

Individual insights can be incredible. Unfortunately, they come at the cost of time—not only to conduct the interviews but to reduce the accumulated findings into a few clear themes that can be acted on or reported to resource providers as *Feedback*.

SWOT 101:

@gapingvoid

Have you ever committed to finishing one of those long restaurant surveys? The kind that suck the life out of you as they bludgeon you with question after question about the food, the server, the bathroom, dessert orders, drink quality, time between arrival and seating and more? People are less inclined to answer surveys—especially long ones—in part because they are less personable than a one-on-one interview, and in part because there is no pressure or requirement to finish them.

At the same time, surveys offer a faster but less detailed method of gathering group-level insight. Surveys can be sent to the entire list of attendees who register for your event as it is occurring, after it is over or both. Surveys do not require a large time investment (especially if you are only looking for trends with number scores). Additionally, participants can take surveys at their convenience—including while waiting to be seated at a restaurant after experiencing your event.

Since people are less responsive to surveys, it can be useful to let them know in the email title of your survey that it is short. It can even be as to-the-point as "Two-Question Survey about (your innovation event name here)." The two questions can be:

1. How likely are you to recommend (your innovation event or process here) to a colleague or friend?

2. Why?

The first question targets the bottom-line metric you are seeking: will your innovation effort grow or decline? I can still recall a moment when one of my MBA professors was lecturing on teamwork, team cohesion and surveys. He talked about how hard it could be for people to be completely honest about their teammates, even if the surveys were anonymous. There was some unmeasurable group of people out in the world who simply did not like to say negative things about other people.

"However," he said, pausing to grin with reflective satisfaction, "there is one question that we began asking teams that told us if they were truly cohesive: 'Would you want to work on this team again?'"

A bottom-line, targeted question can offer insight into a key trend you want to uncover. At AFWERX, we used this question:

Are you likely to recommend attending an AFWERX event to a colleague or friend?

a. No.
b. Would consider.
c. Absolutely!

Rather than using a more traditional three-answer scale such as "Not likely," "Neutral" and "Very likely," the conversational answers helped us collect a big-picture insight while still being a bit more personable. The results probably would not get published in a professional statistics research journal, but we obtained the data we needed to see: an 80 percent "Absolutely" plus a 19 percent "Would consider" and one percent "No" told us what we needed to know.

The big-picture insight is useful, but it does not provide insight into the causes of what makes your innovation effort successful or not so successful. The question "Why?" can help you learn more about your efforts' efficacy. Perhaps you tried something distinct at your innovation event? With all the virtual innovation events appearing since COVID, there are a number of areas for innovating how virtual events are conducted.

In the example above, the first question will not, by itself, reveal the impact of your distinct "experiment." However, adding the second question of "Why?" might. If you ask "Why?" and leave an open comment box, you might learn if your distinct experiment was at the top of the respondents' minds as they reflected on your effort. A survey analyst can look at the comments for trends. Depending on the size of your survey and the number of responses, a single person could read through all the comments in a matter of hours or days. If you have many hundreds of word responses, you might wish to use one of the survey tools technologies (i.e., word clouds, sentiment tags and categorizations) to help uncover the main trends and words being written.

The "Why?" question has its weaknesses as well. Maybe your distinct effort was clever and memorable, but because your keynote speaker was even more compelling, the respondents only focused on her as they wrote their comments. That does not mean your distinct effort did not have an effect—just that it was not the most memorable. To gain insight into the impact of your distinctive effort, an additional survey question focusing on that effort might be necessary, such as:

Did the (distinctive effort name) add value to (insert event or process name)?

Strongly Disagree	Disagree	Neutral	Agree	Strongly Agree
1	2	3	4	5

...and then look to see what is the average from the responses.

Once again, another tradeoff appears. For each new cause that you want to consider, more time is expected from respondents (who generally prefer shorter surveys). Choosing among the many ways to obtain *Feedback* about your *Output* is a bit like choosing what you will play in a game of Rock, Paper, Scissors: each approach has its strengths and weaknesses. In surveys, there are tradeoffs with areas like time commitment, level of detail and causal understanding of your desired big picture outcomes. Experimenting with feedback techniques is its own innovative quest.

YOU aRe only as good as the Love you have foR otheR People.

@gapingvoid

TURNING INWARD FOR FEEDBACK

Most people are pretty familiar with customer *Feedback*, but fewer are familiar with organizational *Feedback*. Sometimes we have the chance to participate in an annual organizational climate survey or some other special interest survey. However, I have participated in countless surveys over the years without seeing any significant changes to my organization as a result.

Organizational *Feedback* needs to be more than an annual survey. If you only talked to your friends once per year—not because you were restricted from talking, but simply because you did not prioritize starting a conversation—would you still be friends in a few years? How can organizational morale or **will** be adjusted if snapshots are only taken once per year? Organizational *Feedback* can be a daily affair, whether it comes from a staff meeting, water cooler talk or individual meetings.

As AFWERX grew from its small team of five to an average

size of about 30 members, I began individual, hour-long gatherings with each of our Capability Leaders (there were 12 or so) every two weeks. The meetings were typically labeled "(Talented Person's name) and Beam Ponder the Universe." I wanted to emphasize how broad and reaching our discussions were allowed to be. Some of our AFWERX Talent played with that title, and if they felt that they would not be offering deep thoughts that week, they would send back an alternative meeting title, such as "(Talented Person's name) and Beam Ponder the Stratosphere."

My side of the agenda was typically non-existent. With a blank slate, I wanted to hear whatever their talented spirit thought was important. Sometimes they began with their tasks and accomplishments. Sometimes they started with a question about a rumor. All *Feedback* was welcomed *Feedback*. This was our time for the WE in AF***WE***RX.

This open, agenda-less gathering format further supported our "centralized intent, decentralized execution" strategy and our *W.A.T.E.R.* culture of empowerment. For example, someone might ask questions about how our general strategy applied to an upcoming decision that they would be making. AFWERX was able to achieve unrivaled growth and impact with our small team because so very little action was held up waiting for the "leader"—me, according to the organizational chart—to approve their decisions.

I deliberately did not request or demand metric updates during the Pondering sessions—we had quarterly OKR checkpoints and monthly briefings to senior leaders for that kind of progress check. I simply started by listening. More than a few confidential sharings, rumors and insights occurred during that time. This also helped prepare me for potential upcoming surprises as our talented members speculated about the future (as a result, I can only recall one "surprise" that had me scrambling when it occurred).

The Pondering sessions also paved the way for boosted team morale. For example, if we had not had deliberate one-on-one meeting times built into our schedules, we may have missed a lot of subtle but pivotal information. Imagine that team member Jack needs Jill to complete something before he can begin some multi-person project, but Jill has not completed her task. Will Jack want to ask for time with me just so that he can complain about Jill for 30 seconds? The "Jill has not finished her task" concern may seem too trivial for requesting a meeting, and so Jack ends up frustrated by Jill and morale suffers. Or worse, Jack lashes out at Jill publicly during a staff meeting, feelings are hurt, different team members pick sides and negative morale impacts our *will*.

However, within the Ponderings structure, by knowing that Jack will meet with me every week or two, he can message Jill's slow responses to me as a mere side story within a larger set of issues. I will make no claim that I resolved 100 percent of all of Jack or Jill's concerns or complaints, but I will write that I was able to quietly resolve a number of disputes and clear up miscommunications because of the Ponderings. One-on-one time between people offers a chance for personal exchanges and trust-building, strengthening the bonds between team members and their mission. Whether you prefer to host daily, weekly or monthly staff meetings, our AFWERX experiences suggest trying some form of agenda-less, individual Ponderings with your team members, project leads, VPs or whomever else.

SURVEYING YOUR INTERNAL TALENT FOR THEIR WILL

Jack and Jill stories are still not a complete *Feedback* method. For example, Jack could be an extrovert and a gossip king who exaggerates the current state of morale or mission challenges. Alternatively, it is possible that Jill or Jack will soft-talk and sugarcoat their concerns until they feel like they can trust you, so they may say "everything is fine" when they are actually feeling stressed out.

In the spring of 2020, AFWERX's success was still continuing to impact our evenings and weekends, so I was looking for specific data I could capture to relay to our senior leaders that we needed more resources to remain sustainable. I did not doubt our *will*, but I was concerned about how our Talent was feeling about what seemed like a constantly increasing pace.

For that reason, I created a short, voluntary anonymous

survey for our AFWERX Talent to complete, allowing them to mark their degree of agreement:

Strongly Disagree	Disagree	Neutral	Agree	Strongly Agree
1	2	3	4	5

...and then also allowed for comment boxes. The seven questions for insight into our collective *will* were:

1. During the last six months, my Capability has been effective in completing its mission.

2. During the last six months, I enjoyed performing my Capability's mission.

3. During the last six months, I enjoyed my work environment.

4. During the last six months, I chose to work more than what was asked of me.

...and as a last, bottom-line question about morale and team *will*, question seven was:

7. I would recommend AFWERX to others as a place to work.

What about Questions 5 and 6, you ask? They required a different set of responses. The questions were:

5. During the last six months, my average hours per week have been:

a. 40-50
b. 50-60
c. 60-70
d. 70-80

6. During the last six months, my mission Capability
ops temp hours have been:

a. Sustainable, 40-60 hours per week, spread across five to
seven days
b. Sustainable, 40-60 hours per week, spread across five days
c. Sustainable, greater than 60 hours per week for two-to-three-
week surges, but then less than 40 hours for others
d. Unsustainable, greater than 60 hours per week for three to
five weeks at a time
e. Unsustainable, greater than 60 hours per week for months at
a time

The results of the survey (100 percent response rate!)
showed that most of our Talent worked more than 40 hours per
week on our mission, and more than a third worked over 60.
Despite this challenging pace, the bottom-line reflection of *will*,
Question 7, showed that 95 percent of our Talent would recommend AFWERX as a place to work to others—and the other 5
percent were simply "Neutral." There were no negative "non-
recommendations."

I discussed our ops tempo with some of AFWERX's senior
leaders and a few months later, something interesting occurred.
In June 2020, AFWERX was combined with other innovation
efforts. In the private sector, it might be said that we were
"bought out," "IPO'ed" or "merger-ed and acquired." However,
rather than calling the new effort "Aggregated Air Force Innovation" or some other new name, the new leadership decided to
name the new, combined innovation effort "AFWERX." That

name selection was a compliment to our Talent and the brand name we had established over three years by being effective for our warfighters and our Air Force. My time for leading AFWERX had come to an end. I stayed on through the summer to help with the transition and accepted an offer to transfer to help with innovation efforts within the Air Force's Strategic Studies Group of the Pentagon.

The days from 2017 to 2020 often felt like each one was a week-long, but when I would look back at a week, it felt as though only a day had passed. It was a very saturating mission, yet through it all we were still able to maintain and build camaraderie, humor and a strong organizational *will*. This is a testament to our incredible Talent, and I also credit the *FLOW* model for helping us focus and organize some of our big picture, not-so-obvious, Common Mind decisions at both the strategic and tactical levels.

Oh, and there is one other nuance within the *FLOW* model that we have not yet been elaborated upon. Do you see it?

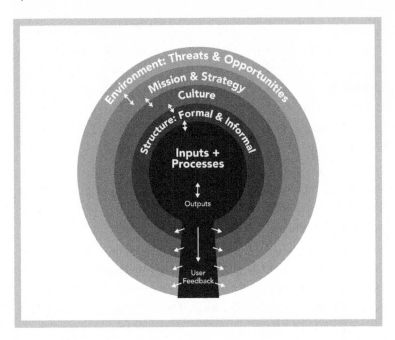

The arrows from *User Feedback* remind us that not only should you <u>obtain</u> *Feedback*, but you should <u>act</u> upon it as well. For example, in 2007, Steve Jobs was looking at Apple Computer's top product lines. As he stated:

"The Mac, iPod, Apple TV and iPhone. Only one of those is a computer, so we're changing the name."

There was a lot packed into those 19 words. Maybe Steve realized that the word "Computer" in the company name might send the wrong signal about priorities or limit people's thinking. The consumer *Environment* had been sending *Feedback* to Apple Computer. Steve reacted to it by renaming "Apple Computer" as "Apple Inc." It was a subtle choice—the kind that left an impression on me and further influenced my inclination to label gatherings as "Ponder the Universe" instead of "one-on-one staff meeting." Words matter.

The experimental mindset used as we were "...building the AFWERX plane while it is already in flight" was one that required actions, feedback and iterations...and then more feedback and iterations. We were constantly adjusting our mission. We never had to change the AFWERX name like Apple did, but we certainly changed our processes and approaches along the way.

Properly conducted, *Feedback* about an *Output* offers a rich set of insights that can influence the ongoing evolution of your innovation effort. The *Feedback* need not merely be external—internal *Feedback* processes and authentic listening also contribute to the *will* of your organization. When properly used and leveraged, *Feedback* and *Output* can place you on a world stage for displaying the talented members and effectiveness of your innovation mission.

INCREASING POSITIVE FLOW WITHIN OUTPUT AND FEEDBACK

*How are you communicating that your innovation actions have a positive ROI for:
-Increasing efficiency
-Increasing effectiveness
-Achieving cost reductions
-Increasing profits (not an *Outcome* for AFWERX nor for most government efforts)

*Is your resource provider—supervisor or senior leader—aware of your innovation's possibilities or recent ROI outcomes? How might you communicate those and increase *will*?

*How will you pursue insights from external stakeholders and participants of your innovation efforts via formal and informal interviews?

*How will you pursue insights from external stakeholders and participants of your innovation efforts via surveys?

*How will you pursue insights from your internal team via formal and informal interviews and Pondering sessions?

*How will you pursue insights from your internal team via surveys?

8

LEADING WITH FLOW:

SISYPHUS INTERVIEWS BEAM

The ancient Greeks told the tale of Sisyphus, a most unique inno-
vator who, among other things, created an initial prototype for how
to cheat death. When his innovative way was not appreciated, Sisy-

phus was judged by the Powers That Be to live in the Underworld and eternally push a rock up a majestic hill, only to see it roll down the other side so that he could follow it down and push it back up the hill.

However, there was a loophole within his punishment sentence. The Judges had ruled that Sisyphus needed to push the rock but not <u>how</u> the rock needed to be pushed. After countless millennia, and seemingly endless conversations with sympathizers as Sisyphus pushed his rock, the sympathizers were able to create and gift Sisyphus an infinite energy, rock-pushing machine. With his physical presence no longer required to push the boulder, Sisyphus began to pick up new hobbies in the underworld—including podcasting. After considering his own struggles, he thought that I might be a compatible guest for an interview. The transcript from our gathering follows:

S: Welcome, everyone, to another podcast of *Upon This Rock*. I am here today with one of the co-founders of AFWERX, Dr. Brian "Beam" Maue, who was also the AFWERX Mission Leader during their startup years. We are going to explore with him the amazing rise of AFWERX onto the national and global stage as a force for innovation. Welcome to the show, Beam!

B: Thank you for the invitation, Sisyphus, and for the chance to share this story of our incredible airmen and our Air Force making our nation stronger through greater agility.

S: Glad you accepted the invite, Beam. Are you ready to rock?

B: Ready to roll!

S: Then let's get to it. Let's start with AFWERX's recent ranking as one of the Best Workplaces for Innovators in the world— number 16 on the list. This seems like the first time a government-led organization has made that kind of a list. Can you tell us a bit about what that meant to AFWERX?

LIFe,
LIBeRTY,
AND THe
PURSUIT
OF OUR
HIGHeST
SeLveS.

@gapingvoid

B: Great question! AFWERX was created to drive innovation that would help secure our nation's future. Our focus for our first three years was to create warfighter agility—options at the speed of relevance—by empowering airmen with innovative processes and opportunities. Their success was our success, and it was a thrill to see our airmen recognized for their world-class talent.

S: I bet the mortals were glad to see that taxpayer dollars received a world class capability in return. I'm curious—were there any other organizations on that list who were a comparison organization for AFWERX?

B: The official answer is "No," Sisyphus—our government *Environment* and bureaucratic constraints are so distinct that any actual comparison with the private sector would be like comparing apples to oranges, and the government is neutral with regard to private industry dealings.

S: That makes sense, Beam. So, do you have an "unofficial answer?" Maybe a favorite fruit from within the fruit bowl?

B: You are placing me between a rock and a hard place, Sisyphus. Hmm...an "off the record," not-typically-spoken-in-public kind of fruit?

S: ...that would be heard with neutral, non-favoritism ears by our *Upon This Rock* community.

B: Well then, one of the Founding Fathers of AFWERX was the

second highest ranking general in the Air Force—Vice Chief of Staff General Wilson. During more than a few meetings, he would offer his vision of what he wanted AFWERX to achieve, such as, "Beam, one day it would be great if some of the folks over at Amazon looked at AFWERX and said, 'I wish we could be a little more like AFWERX.'" That was the standard he was asking us to achieve. It was also a compliment to Amazon. So, when the Fast Company rankings of 2020 went public, it was a little bit satisfying to be just a smidge above Amazon on the rankings list.

S: You felt like you had achieved General Wilson's goal?

B: Let us just agree that I felt as though our AFWERX efforts had been "fruitful."

S: (groaning) I am picking up a vibe that you like puns and similes.

B: It is possible that my combined decade of leading Cub Scouts and teaching tired military cadets forged a communication style mixed with gravitas and buffoonery.

S: Speaking of gravitas, I noticed that you mentioned General Wilson as a "Founding Father." Did you model AFWERX with America's founding in mind?

B: Yes indeed. Our Nation's founding, with our colonies-turned-states each having such distinct, independent approaches to their development, was a great simile for discussing our strategy of empowerment-of-personal-strengths—Abraham Maslow also inspired. Additionally, we at AFWERX used a limited central authority governance and supported maximum empowerment of our frontline innovators—the classic "centralized intent, decentralized execution" approach that works well in certain *Environments*.

S: Nice...

B: Oh! I could also explain AFWERX using a Zen simile or riddle. Are you up for that?

S: You're asking me, a guy who has been rolling a rock uphill for the better part of eternity, if I am "up" for something?

B: My apologies, Sisyphus. I did not mean to go there.

S: It's all good, Beam. I've made peace with my choices and consequences. Besides, as a result of my clever behavior, I'm given a break every now and then to host this podcast about success through purposeful persistence and innovation.

B: In that case, here is the riddle: How do you control a large herd?

S: Hmmm...how do you control a large herd? I don't know. How?

B: The answer is...give it a lot of space. Can you imagine what would happen if you fenced in a large herd of cattle in a way that required each bull with pointy horns to be placed shoulder-to-shoulder against each other? With nowhere for them to wander, how long would it take until tempers started flaring up? Until horns started poking into different neighbors—on accident at first but then in retaliation and on purpose? Pretty soon, stampede!

For an AFWERX comparison, I tried to give each of our "large talents" plenty of room to roam so that they could build up their Capabilities based on their strengths. Stated negatively, I was superconscious about *not* micromanaging our talented AFWERX members and *not* forcing them to fit into some constraining, limited vision that my mind had created. I usually put the word "leader" in air quotes when I speak about my role at AFWERX. Perhaps "shepherd" would have been

more appropriate. "Controlling dictator" would be inappropri-
ate. I did not drive innovation. I shepherded, empowered and
drove the herd that drove innovation.

S: Beam, you just connected a 20th century, Western civilization
business school insight with Zen advice that is millennia old.
Do you do that often?

B: Maybe, Sisyphus, but fusing together wisdom from different
times with a common principle is not unique to me. Do you
remember President Ronald Reagan's speech from the 1988
State of the Union address?

S: Like it was five minutes ago. Which part?

B: The part where President Reagan said:

> *"History records the power of the ideas that brought us here those
> seven years ago. Ideas like the individual's right to reach as far and as
> high as his or her talents will permit, the free market as an engine of
> economic progress and, as an ancient Chinese philosopher, Lao Tzu,
> said, 'Govern a great nation as you would cook a small fish; do not
> overdo it.'"*

Change out "seven years" with "three years" and "nation"
with "AFWERX" and you have a pretty good insight into my
shepherding style. I guided AFWERX in accordance with 7,000
years of timeless principles that had influenced me, such as
from Lao Tzu and another of his statements from 2,400 years
ago written in his book, *Tao Te Ching*. Teacher Lao stated:
"When the great leader's work is done, the people will say 'We
did it ourselves.'"

Stated negatively, "If a leader is lousy, the people will speak
of the leader's oppressions daily." I tried to "shepherd"
AFWERX with some general guidance about direction and

fields of interest, but I tried to leave as much roaming and deci-sion-making space available as possible for our AFWERX Talent—they knew how to best optimize for their capability area. I think a more modern day, less riddle-like, saying would be, "Surround yourself with trustworthy people smarter than yourself and let them do their jobs."

S: ...but you must have done something during your time besides trust your people. What are some of the ways you were able to "lead" without leading?

B: To "lead without leading" is a subtle act, and I make no claim that I achieved that standard all of the time. However, when I was successful at it, you would observe that I really sought to maximize individual space on each of our talented members' calendars. To elaborate a bit, every week I tried to project forward two weeks and communicate key milestones or

upcoming events that required our Talent to produce something. Since we were distributed across four time zones, that
usually meant crafting an email, which I tried to inject with
positive *FLOW* energy via purposeful *Mission* insights, historical *Environment* facts or even best practices relating to happiness *Processes*...and maybe a groan-able pun or two.

I also used the *FLOW* model to scan the *Environments* of the
Pentagon and national defense news, as well as formulate feedback discussions with our Vice Chief, General Wilson. By
providing our AFWERX Talent with plenty of vision and time
for key activities, they were allowed to roam and prioritize their
days and weeks in pursuit of how they best thought their efforts
would help Air Force innovation. They were in control of their
capability areas and their own calendars.

I can only recall one time when I needed to ask for something within a 72-hour time frame because I had not realized
that some priority was coming due. Otherwise, with the exception of COVID actions or a few other moments that were out of
my control, I did not have to "lead" anyone to change their
priorities or adjust their lives. There was not a whole lot of
"Stop what you are doing! Adjust your actions to me, your
leader!" kind of micromanagement.

S: Did you view the fields of opportunity with more than a two-
week time span?

B: Indeed. For example, during quarterly Common Mind gatherings, within the first hour I would often bring up a story or
two about the *Environment*, such as some of the atrocities
committed by Communist governments—an element of their
threat is real, and it shows signs of increasing aggression.

Those news clips and historical reminders would set the

stage for a review of our *Mission and Strategy,* as well as our *Culture.* The *Culture* segment was particularly fun because by our second year, that part of our gathering usually had one or two of our talented members performing magic tricks—some of which were Cub Scout level quality, while others were semi-professional. These three factors of *FLOW* review took under 30 minutes to cover and connected the diverse Talent within our Common Mind to our shared experiences. We could then focus on our other AFWERX-wide issues for the next day or two with our connective bonds strengthened. Those Common Mind gatherings were a unique creation for our AFWERX efforts...even the Common Mind gathering name was about the fusion of our "we."

Additionally, I cannot think of any time when I had to make or "lead" our Talent collectively, say or do something that they did not believe in. Maybe there were some changes to some project messaging or a reprioritization of where resources went, but there was not a whole lot of "leading" because the Talent was already headed to those particular fields of interest anyway. I worked hard to create an open transparent environment so that most efforts generally had an agreed-upon direction. Very rarely did I actually have to be a deciding tiebreaker, and when I was, there was transparency behind why I chose what I did.

Lastly, I think it is important to note that I was able to use the large herd approach to shepherding because key senior leaders—General Wilson, Lieutenant General Harris, senior executive (Jack) Blackhurst—*never* gave AFWERX a specific task with a specific timeline or method for how some objective needed to be accomplished. Their big herd leadership style was beneficial to our *Mission* speed and agility.

S: Leading without leading...advice that has stood the test of time from the days of Lao Tzu.

B: I am biased, Sisyphus. I tend to think that if something is still being discussed after a thousand or more years, it is probably not a silly fad. I bet you have seen a few fads in your time.

S: I bet I have seen 99 percent of them.

B: Did you have a favorite language fad that has come and gone?

S: Shiver me timbers, Matey! That be talking like a pirate, especially for speakin' of the bilge rats who came up with thee 1970s shag carpet.

B: Nicely articulated, ya scurvy dog. What about a most memorable versus faddish phrase from your Ancient Greece that can still be seen today?

S: *Molon Labe*![1]

B: A most excellent choice from 300 options.

S: Most exemplary, indeed. Hey, speaking of options, do you have any other pain points for which you wish you could wave a magic wand and make disappear?

B: Hmmm...I believe so. Sometimes, we are our one worst enemy, Sisyphus.

S: Have you been talking to my friend Oedipus, Beam?

B: He screwed up royally, yes? More seriously, Sisyphus, we started AFWERX at the same time that our government leaders wanted to see more innovation from our military. For example, the *Summary of 2018 National Defense Strategy* specifically noted that "Delivering performance means we will shed outdated management practices and structures while integrating insights from business innovation."

With that guidance in mind, we began planning an event that included offering a commemorative T-shirt purchase option—the kind that innovation businesses ordinarily do at these kinds of events. The design of our T-shirt had already been made earlier in the year, when we expected to have an in-person event and wanted to have an easy way to distinguish the AFWERX crew members who were allowed to touch equipment. There were no additional taxpayer dollars that were going to be spent on creating these shirts. We then set up an optional web link to a third-party T-shirt vendor. Somehow, a project review team concluded that "the optics did not look good" and our T-shirt web link was shut down after just three days. As a contrast, over 100 T-shirt purchasers thought that the optics did look good during those three days before the website was shut down. Additionally, not a single taxpayer complaint was received.

...and then, about two weeks later, there was another innovation event by another defense organization, and there were plenty of T-shirts available for sale. Apparently, their project review team had a more innovation-friendly interpretation of what "integrating insights from business innovation" meant. Government innovation should not be so arbitrary. When innovation efforts are arbitrarily stopped by review teams, the *will* of the mission members to give up extra evenings and weekends away from family and friends is definitely weakened.

S: It sounds to me like that review team had zero tolerance for anything but the safe play. It if wasn't written down somewhere, then they were afraid to try it.

B: That review team demonstrated a zero-risk tolerance...and even the word "risk" in that cliché sounds far more ominous than the reality. Would Congress actually shut down AFWERX over an optional T-shirt being sold by a separate, non-AFWERX affiliated business?

S: I have been around the block a few times...

B: You mean up and down the hill.

S: Whatever. I have seen, and can hear, the old way of bureaucratic thinking: "Better safe than sorry" and "No one ever got fired for punting on fourth down."

B: Sure, but from *what* was it that the review team was keeping us safe? AFWERX had already been hosting events for over two years, with well over 2,000 people in attendance and no one—

not one—ever wrote a complaint about excessive waste or misuse of government funds. Our feedback was overwhelmingly positive. Why did the review committees fear Congress over a T-shirt?

S: That is interesting data. Okay, so speaking of Congress, what would you like Congress or anyone else to do to advance government innovation efforts, whether at the federal or any other governmental level?

We are more scared of being wrong than we are scared of going our whole life without creating anything

@gapingvoid

B: There are some factors within the *Environment* that would make government innovation easier if changed. My top five list in no particular order would be:

    1. Congressional language that would allow "marketing activities" for innovation events and missions, such as the creation of souvenir T-shirts. Additionally, language

that allows "use of commonly accepted innovation event practices" during events that have innovation activities occurring. For example, the offering of light refreshments and food to attendees has been a best business practice precedent. Without food, people leave an innovation event in search of food and collaboration opportunities are lost, decreasing the effectiveness of the event.

2. Congressional language could set aside a certain amount of money for military innovation. The amount could be "low risk" by congressional standards— perhaps $100 million per military service per year. The money would be labeled as innovation funds and could be spent however it needs to be spent, with an end-of-year report being sent to Congress. Currently, government innovation efforts are hampered because some projects are seen as research-oriented while others are seen as operations or maintenance-oriented. Each of those types of innovations require a special type of money. The need to find the right type of money slows down government innovation—organizations rarely have all of the right types of the needed quantities. Types of money create constraints that give an advantage to our nation's adversaries by reducing our agility. We need innovation money without money type constraints.

3. Require that each government organization with a large annual budget—perhaps $500 million or more—set aside three percent of its budget for new innovative experimentation. This will cause "creative destruction" as outdated programs must fade out and be closed, and new improvement processes must be attempted.

4. Allow for the purchase of labor to help run innovation projects for a few months at a time. The ideal labor

pool for AFWERX would be military reservists and guardsmen, who represent the best of the business world and the military ethos. The hiring steps for these members is currently based on outdated guidance that does not allow instant hiring for innovation, but instead is usually a "back fill" for some active-duty member who is deployed. Reservists are so much more than "back fill" bench sitters!

5. Create stronger innovation incentives for government members. For example, if organizations are able to show that they are more innovative, half of the savings demonstrated could be kept by the organization and placed within their annual budget to be distributed to team members as bonuses and gratitude. This would further motivate government members to keep looking for innovative ways to make America's government better.

...and again, we do not just need Congress—we need to clean up some of our own risk-aversions. We need more leaders willing to empower their skilled teams. I have seen some organizations with generals who wanted to personally approve expenses as small as $25,000. Why not trust your talented people with purchases under $50,000 or $100,000? Gaining a general's approval might take a week or longer, and a decision-making cycle of once per week is not agile.

S: It does not seem like you are breaking any big eggs to make a better innovation omelette for America's government, Beam.

B: The difference between "man's laughter" and "man-slaughter" is a minor rearrangement of a few ingredients, but sometimes seemingly little actions yield drastic effects, Sisyphus. In general, Congress or senior DoD leaders can help any time they encourage project approval authorities to live by a code of "If it is not declared illegal and you could confidently tell your grandma or children what you are doing with a clean conscience, then you may try this prototyping experiment."

S: Powerful. Alright, what kind of ingredients and background does someone need in order to join an innovation team?

B: Within our AFWERX *Mission*, we would accept just about anyone with a track record for innovating, an interest to learn and a willingness to help people—and who humbly accept that sometimes boring grunt work must be accomplished.

S: Sure, but is there a preferred technical background?

B: A technical background was not needed for AFWERX, but it may be for other innovation organizations, depending upon their *Mission* objectives. For our AFWERX *Mission*, it was more important that we were able to connect innovators with results-producing people and processes.

S: I appreciate the emphasis on moving the ball forward to achieve results. We are nearing the end of our time, so let's move on from the past to the future. What are your predictions for the "new" AFWERX—let's call it "AFWERX 2.0," the one that you helped transition as you were leaving in the summer of 2020?

B: Sisyphus, some things in life are unsatisfying, like the first time you try to eat cold, day-old fast food French fries. My answer to this question will probably also be unsatisfying, because my answer is "it depends." If I may tangent for just a second?

S: I do prefer edgy...

B. Thanks. I remember how unsatisfied a reporter was when I gave her a long "it depends" answer to her question of, "So, Beam, where you are going to build the next AFWERX innovation hub? Boston? Seattle?"

I responded to that reporter:

"That is a great question. AFWERX was built upon the same supply and demand principles that guided the evolution of humanity, particularly from Age of Enlightenment thinkers such as Adam Smith writing in *The Wealth of Nations* and Alexis de Tocqueville's thoughts in *Democracy in America*. AFWERX was also built through debates on the merits of self-interest that occurred between Aristotle and Plato thousands of years ago. In total, we have tried to integrate about 7,000 years' worth of insights into our design. At our core, AFWERX seeks to help our airmen solve their pain points as well as take advantage of opportunities, and so we respond to the 'demand signal' with whatever our airmen need. As a result, if they need a new innovation hub in Boston, then we will build one in Boston. If they need more Spark Cells, then we will build more Spark Cells. It depends upon the demand signal."

As I spoke, I thought that I heard angelic harps begin to play. While I pontificated upon neo-classical economic models, I believe that I saw at least two older gentlemen a few feet away begin to weep. I think they were both economists. "So," concluded the reporter as she raised her recording device to her lips, "You do not have a plan..." and she clicked off her recording device.

S: You are making that up!

B: It is true.

S: No way!

B: Way! And to finish answering your question, as AFWERX 2.0 began in the summer of 2020, the veterans of the AFWERX 1.0 did our best to articulate to the new leadership what had been successful for us during our startup years, including by providing our Common Mind summary of Historical Strengths and our Ideal Future. AFWERX 2.0 was projected to have more people, more resources and more senior leadership supporting it. Since we were departing AFWERX with it operating at a level of performance that was ranked #16 in the world, we felt like AFWERX 2.0 had a good chance for success.

S: That makes sense, although innovation is not something your command-and-control military is known for—at least not when compared to the flexible, out-of-a-garage, entrepreneurial startup.

B: *Au contraire mon frère,* much of history has been written by innovative militaries. You of all people should be familiar with the story of the Trojan Horse.

S: The Greeks know how to pick a winning pony.

B: Legends may grow over time, but whether that horse was 10 feet tall and had one Greek hidden in it or 30 feet tall holding 10 Greeks, some kind of deception happened after that horse was rolled into the city of Troy. Something happened the night the Trojans celebrated their perceived victory over the Greeks. Somebody—whether from within the horse or a traitor from Troy's population or a sneaky small team that went undetected during the Trojans' drunken celebration—was able to open the gates for the Greeks. I do not think Odysseus just made the whole thing up. Archeologists believe that Troy existed. History was forever altered, somehow, and a wooden horse innovation was somehow involved.

Innovation—even within command-and-control *Environments*—is scattered throughout military history. Hannibal and his elephants crossing the Alps comes to mind. Sun Tzu, who noted that the acme of skill was to win a war without needing to go to battle, was incredibly big on innovative actions as well.

S: I can see that. So, which military innovation or campaign has AFWERX been most like?

B: Washington crossing the Delaware River on Christmas night en route to a surprise attack on the Hessian forces located in Trenton, New Jersey.

S: And why is that?

B: It was not because of some incredible unique technology that Washington won that battle on December 26th. It was because he thought and acted differently: armies did not normally campaign in the wintertime. AFWERX thought and acted differently during our startup years: innovation never sleeps (but we should!). Another parallel from Washington's mission was that much of his plan did not reach fruition. He arrived at the battle with a much smaller force than expected, in part due to a disruptive winter storm *Environment*. AFWERX was a small team, and we certainly encountered obstacles that prevented the full measure of our efforts from being realized, yet we still succeeded. I could go on, but the main point is that the *FLOW* of thought and action that brought General Washington and the Continental Army success was much like how AFWERX worked within the *FLOW* to achieve innovation success.

S: I like it—Washington and the Continentals helped secure a new nation one battle at a time, and AFWERX has been out there empowering airmen and securing innovation's future one relationship at a time and one project at a time. Beam, it has been a real pleasure learning a bit more about AFWERX and successful government innovation. Before you go, I have a little game that I like to play with our guests called "What would Silent Cal say?"

B: Is this the same Silent Cal who was President Calvin Coolidge? The same Silent Cal who, when a person seated next to him at a dinner party began with, "I made a bet today that I could get more than two words out of you," President Coolidge replied, "You lose"?

S: The very same.

B: I am so ready for this...bring it.

S: Alrighty, I will give you President Coolidge's opening lines and you must fill in the blank. Here we go:

"Nothing in this world can take the place of persistence. Talent will not—"

B: "Nothing is more common than unsuccessful men with talent."

S: "Genius will not—"

B: "Unrewarded genius is almost a proverb!"

S: "Education will not—"

B: "The world is full of educated derelicts."

S: "Persistence and determination alone are omnipotent—"

B: "The slogan 'Press On!' has solved and always will solve the problems of the human race."

S: It was if you were reading my mind, Beam.

B: Almost a Common Mind, Sisyphus...

9

CONCLUSION:

THREE VIEWS FROM THE MOUNTAIN

Climbing a mountain remains a timeless metaphor for innovators. Themes of struggle and perseverance spring to mind, and in the case of our friend Sisyphus from the last chapter, sometimes you finish a great effort only to see it undone by circumstances beyond your control and are left with no choice but to start all over again. Tests of character abound within innovation efforts, and AFWERX was no exception.

However, there are also moments of triumph within an innovation effort where you may pause to enjoy the view of the progress that you have helped create, whether you are at the summit or not. Although hindsight might be 20/20 (a great pun in the year 2020, when there was not too much to joke about), I wish to continue to apply selective vision and conclude our journey together with three views that seem most applicable to this moment within our exploration.

1. "I HAVE THE HAPPINESS TO KNOW THAT IT IS A RISING, NOT A SETTING, SUN..."

At the conclusion of the drafting of the US Constitution,

Benjamin Franklin remarked about a sun that was molded onto the back of Gen George Washington's chair. From Franklin's point of view, that sun had seemed to be setting during times of Constitutional Convention struggle, such as when state representatives were debating over how various-sized states should be represented in Congress. Franklin also admitted that he had felt like the sun was rising whenever constitutional progress was being achieved. As the Constitution writing conference was ending, Franklin was pleased to note that it was a rising sun on the back of Washington's chair...a new nation had been given life.

That life had an interesting birthday. Have you ever wondered why the United States celebrates July 4, 1776, as our birthday? We could very easily have celebrated October 19, 1781, as our nation's day of independence, which was the day when the colonies and the French achieved victory over Gen Charles Cornwallis and his British troops and secured US independence. Alternatively, we could have celebrated our nation's birthday on September 3, 1783, when the Treaty of Paris "officially" recognized us as the United States of America. Yet our predecessors chose the Fourth of July.

What an incredible historical precedent for America—commemorating the value of "the idea" as our nation's birth. On that day, our Founding Fathers declared our unalienable rights to "Life, Liberty and the pursuit of Happiness," and then many would risk life and fortune (and many would lose both) to create our unique country of innovation within the world. Our nation celebrates its unique heritage based on the moral idea of an individual's worth and the subsequent conclusion that governments should receive their powers from the consent of the governed (who are individuals of worth).

The Founding Fathers were not perfect. Indeed, some of their flaws would create conditions for the Civil War during our young nation's first century. Yet despite our predecessors' flaws, within 200 years their system of "startup" colonies would start small, fail fast and often learn quickly, scale bigger and win big (including during two World Wars) to become a global superpower, a moon lander and a prosperity leader.

For historical purposes, July 5, 2017, is the AFWERX Independence Day. Before that, many representatives and stakeholders for AFWERX were assembling, but much like the Declaration of Independence, the aggregation and unification of efforts (if a bit clunky) were not solidified and announced until July 5. It would have been July 4, but we were busy honoring our nation's startup history.

That history contains some incredible truths. Now, there are many paths to Truth with a capital "T," but only one destination. During our AFWERX startup years, a view of Truth that appeared again and again was how incredibly progress-oriented America has been, even for those working within large, bureaucratic institutions. The Founding Fathers gave us much to reflect upon, including that:

*Our "Life" is a gift, filled with the good fortune of living in America. This *Environment* for our lives is a privilege and responsibility. Defending the American way, whether in military uniform or as a private citizen, is a cause worthy of our time.

*Our "Liberty" is a gift—America is distinctive for the way so many people have been able to take their ideas and create world-altering businesses, in part because our government allows for innovative experiments and business growth from anyone willing to try. AFWERX was started within a traditional command-and-control system, yet given a large amount of liberty by which to create our capabilities.

*Our "pursuit of Happiness" is a gift—how many people in how many nations never even get to choose whether they can work hard to produce something great? AFWERX required tremendous commitment, but since we were given a worthy cause and the autonomy to act and achieve purposeful outcomes, a sense of fulfillment and happiness was almost inevitable (and was reflected in our AFWERX climate survey data!).

The ideas forming AFWERX were similar to those that formed the US Constitution: create a framework of possibilities capable of evolving and uniting efforts that produce reality-altering impacts. We may have made mistakes, but collectively WE of AF*WE*RX—whether our core Talent or the tens of thousands of airmen, entrepreneurs, venture capitalists, academics and industry-minded allies—answered a call to make our Air Force and our nation more agile and capable.

May the sun continue to rise for AFWERX!

2. SAYING "UNTIL NEXT TIME…"

If you understand that AF***WE***RX was built upon a WE philosophy that operated with an awareness of *FLOW* and the *will*, then you will likely understand that to place my "thank you" into some separate section of the book, such as acknowledgments, would violate the 7,000 years of principles upon which our AFWERX startup years were built. For that reason, I offer you an excerpt from my "Until next time.." letter that I wrote and sent to our AFWERX Talent as I was preparing to leave:

Dear Diverse Talent within our Common Mind,

Thank You!

…if, as the research suggests, people are most inclined to

remember the beginning and the end of a communication, then if you only remember one thought from this Common Mind message, may it be my thanks to you for the incredible 3+ years of building AFWERX together!

No one travels a journey like AFWERX—if there are other quests such as ours (?)—alone, and so I would like to express my gratitude to some of our amazing Talent who also spent a lot of extra time offering me strategic insights, considerations and fellowship during our startup years. Weekends and late nights might be part of the startup culture, but to invest so many with others who are committed to the cause made me realize over time that:

"The WE inspired when we should have been tired..."

...and so, I wish to thank:

*Mark "Daggers" Ingram: He wrote the first AFWERX concept paper in 2017...and then 12 more, representing our first prototype-and-iterate project, even before AFWERX launched! From that moment on, if it was important, Daggers and I shared a Common Mind for it—decisions, presentations, etc.

To be historically clear, Daggers performed this Common Mind Meld with me over and above his budget shuffles with Wolf, which kept AFWERX alive financially even as his Business Process creations made us faster and deflected the never-ending inquiries, as well as...well, endless Goodness and Strength. We were also supposed to take turns caring for Schrödinger's cat, but we were never quite sure about its existence...

*Mark "Rocketeer" Rowland: A few years ago, some small-minded f_ _ _ s who shall go unnamed issued me an ultimatum: "Beam, lay down your principles and sever ties with Mark Rowland, or else..."

(you placed " e̲ a̲ r̲ " in those blanks, yes?)

I replied "Molon Labe!" ...and the onslaught did come—"coincidental" complaints that resulted in investigations, a campaign of disrepute, threats of firing and broader ripples that slowed down our mission. To those who endured and cleverly joined in the counterpunch—thank you, again. You never flinched...steadfast in our cause...

If I were given the chance, I would make the same choice again. Rocketeer's world class skills started shaping us in 2017, when he guided our first "What would AFWERX look like?" gathering with our small team, and he has consistently elevated our Common Mind and performance while giving our AF Senior Leaders, the DoD (including the Defense Innovation Board) and our Nation hope for government-business partnerships.

Side note: The upswing from "under assault" to #16 prompted a T-shirt phrase within me:

Sweet #16 Common Mind

Defeats

Small-minded F__ __ __ s

(e̲ a̲ r̲)

...this may become an actual T-shirt. Perhaps I shall post it on a third-party website, sell it for no profit and...oh, wait...

...continuing the gratitude fluidity...

*Tony "Queso" Perez: Started with nothing, cultivated a WE of Common Mind to develop over 70 Spark Cells. Incredible bi-weekly strategic, tactical and occasional buffoonery exchanges occurred within our Common Mind time. Vice Chief even coined him after one of our VCSAF updates.

*Vince "Swath" Pecoraro: Started with nothing, kept AFWERX alive with only the power of his ideas, because he had to renounce his contracting superpowers in exchange for joining our Common Mind. His WE cultivations have expanded minds ranging from singular projects to entire base rebuilds.

*Craig "Yogi" Leavitt: Started with nothing, developed a MAJCOM innovation program that became a major source of cross-cutting project work for our AFWERX challenges while at the same time cultivated a WE of innovators at the many AF headquarters, giving our Common Mind massive applicability insight.

*Cindy "Prohibition" Schurr: Sun Tzu wrote much of the value of spies and information, including that "Defeating an enemy without battle is the acme of skill." Prohibition provided a lot of insights to our Common Mind that won battles without confrontation, well before any battle lines would be drawn.

*Jorge "Rhinestone" Manresa: Started with nothing (sensing a trend?) and continues to work to build a RAPIDX capability that will revolutionize AF innovation. Despite delays to RAPIDX resourcing, he cultivates a WE for our Common Mind that includes a *Coalition of the Willing* in the form of skillful contracting officers—teaching others to fish while making our AF more agile.

*Matthew "FUban" Scott: Started with nothing—maybe even started with a negative balance on Capital Factory's ledgers—and has cultivated an incredible WE of AFWERX-Austin (including Swag, what a win for us!) to create impacts from projects to SBIR to Spark Tank to Joint Services to SXSW to...their enhancement of our Common Mind amazes...

*Charles "Top Secret" Perla: Started our very first hub of AFWERX-DC and brings collegiality and analytic genius to our AFWERX Challenges, Pentagon presentations, SBIR development and more. From lunches to losses (in chess, for me), what a great collaborative skill within our Common Mind.

*Tina "WAG" Parker: Started with a "something (Thanks, Kicks! Thanks, SnaQ!)," and helped further cultivate a WE of Common Mind marketing and messaging that would earn numerous Top Headlines on Air Force messaging platforms, do battle for us against the Forces of Fear and continues to focus us.

*Kehndog, YouTube, Storm and the rest of *theDifference*: From our very first Fusion project—where we once again performed a pivot-and-iteration from "Drone Warz" to "Perimeter Security"—to the recent revolutions and world record setting for the Agility Prime "flying cars" project, *theDifference's* positive strengths-based building blocks and "find a way to yes" have produced world class effects not ever seen before within the DoD...or U.S. Government.

I have broken the Pentagon standard of "one screen page" for messages, but since this is an optional read, and there are more Talented Spirits for whom I give thanks, I concisely group praise:

Big D

Freebie

Laz

Quick Draw

Scrub

Webb

Brad L

GoW

LEAFF

Rambeaux

Senator

Wolf

Brian D

Greg H

Matt V

Razor

SnaQ

X-Lax

Bubbles

Hobo

NAPA

Reboot

Special K

Zen

Carrie M

Hulk

Narnia

Redo

Stinker Pants

Zipper

Catfish

J Flynn

Nate K

Robin

Swag

Crash

Kicks

Patch

Ross

Thor

Cupcake

King

Penguin

Sade

TW

DJ

Kyle

Phil F

Sarah G

Twitch

Eddie

Elmo

inevitably, I missed some Diverse Talent, and for that, I ask for forgiveness...WE built this...low ego, problem solvers for warfighters...an incredible WE experience...

This is a pivotal chapter in AFWERX's story, and you are its authors. I can see how a Fusion event could be an Agility Prime topic of interest, coinciding with a SBIR cycle that is bolstered from Spark Cells connectivity and possibly early foreshadowing at Spark Tank. So many possibilities...continue to look out for each other, and the Goodness will continue...

To paraphrase from Edmund Burke, "The only thing necessary for the triumph of evil is for good people to do nothing." The threat to our future is real, dear Talented Spirits. Thank you for choosing to act...

Be fluid, stay agile and I shall see you from another side,

AFX-5 out...in the act of alternate reality creation...

3. WHY THIS BOOK WAS WRITTEN

Over 2,400 years ago, the ancient Greek author Herodotus, regarded by many as the "Father of History," wrote *The Histories*. What else could it have been titled? It is Western civilization's first major history book and it begins this way:

"This is a presentation of the inquiry of Herodotus of Halicarnassus, which is made so that the deeds of mankind shall not become faded away through time, and so works both great and wonderful shall not be without fame..."

AFWERX did not seek fame during our startup years; WE sought to help solve warfighter capability challenges through a demand-supply-bridge system. We never sought an award as part of our mission, but it was nice to be externally recognized as **#16 in the world** out of 865 organizations evaluated by Fast Company in 2020. However, as the first wave of AFWERX members started to move on to other assignments, I did not want our lessons learned and key considerations to be lost to the ages. Our *FLOW* of actions may help other government innovators, or innovators more generally, with their establishment or execution of an innovation mission and the *will* to succeed.

If you would like a deeper, more tactical view of our AFWERX approaches during our startup years, you may find them on the web by keyword searching for our ebook written during AFWERX's second year, *AFWERX: Empowering Next Generation Innovators and Innovations*. If you cannot find it, write to me at the address below and I will send you a copy.

This book was also a fusion of Goodness that was elevated to an entirely higher realm by two additional allies. First, Jason Korman and the culture design group at Gapingvoid. Not only have I benefited from insightful discussions with Jason, he and GV worked with me to enhance my writings with their Culture Graphics (more formally "Semiotics"). I saw GV's effectiveness firsthand when they were involved in multiple Air Force innovation projects relating to organizational culture. GV's ability to demonize negative behaviors in a non-threatening way while promoting positive actions led to some amazing impacts—in some cases, a 100x increase in motivated engagement by an organization (memorable!). If a picture is worth a thousand words, then much of this book's tale has been elaborated upon by GV's thought-provoking depictions of meaning.

Additionally, I want to express my gratitude to Anna David and the team at Launch Pad Publishing for being able to answer the question, "Who should I trust with one of the most important ideas of my life?" Ryan "Wolverine" Aliapoulios was a Mind of the Universe editor who offered reflections from Albert Camus with the same casual ease that he offered his research from YouTube videos. Kaitlin "eBEAM" Anthony (yes, another BEAM...who knew?) energetically crafted with care everything from detailed book formatting to this final, meta-level creation. Heidi "River" Le flowed magic into the visible and the behind-the-scenes activities that made *The Experiment That Succeeded* possible. Finally, Anna "Dancer" David—NY Times best-selling author and subtle sage who appreciated the space between "Godiva" and "Go Diva,"—responded "Yes" to this proposal when others would have thought "Government innovation? Oxymoron. Pass..." Her range of vision made this process an expansive, enjoyable journey.

Lastly, I give thanks to my family. Karin, Sarah, Noah, Isaiah, Lucah and Jonah all accepted (tolerated?) that I would not be around as much for a few years so that I could help secure our family's future and our nation's future by driving innovation. Families sacrifice much in support of our nation, and I am incredibly thankful for the energizing spirit that mine offered me during the shepherding of AFWERX and earlier military duties and assignments.

AFWERX is no longer an experiment, and it is my hope that the deeds of AFWERX—from core members and allies alike—when viewed from the *FLOW* perspective and the accompanying factor questions, will help give you and your organization a better ability to generate the necessary *will* to make your innovation effort successful, even in the face of challenging climbs.

One last quote from Lao Tzu and the *Tao Te Ching* seems proper:

> *Under heaven, nothing is softer or more yielding than water.*
> *Yet for attacking the solid and strong, nothing is better than*
> *water.*

Water—soft, yielding, flowing water—carved out the Grand Canyon within those rigid rocks of Arizona. Not overnight, but with time. The creators and contributors of AFWERX have started a new *FLOW* within our rather rigid government bureaucracy, and with time, ours and others' efforts will combine and carve out a new, more innovative reality for our nation's future.

Tuebor,

~Beam, 2020

beam@escapethecave.life

NOTES

8. Leading with FLOW:

1. "Come and take them," spoken by King Leonidas in response to Xerxes I asking Leonidas's outnumbered Spartan army to throw down their weapons at the Battle of Thermopylae.

ABOUT THE AUTHOR

Brian E. A. "Beam" Maue, PhD co-founded and led AFWERX, a new US Air Force organization established to empower its people to create greater cultural agility and technological capabilities. Beam's diverse earlier travels include developing hypersonic and nuclear missile options, advancing diplomacy through US treaty efforts and teaching at the US Air Force Academy's Management Department. Through his myriad service to his country, he has honed his signature "eudemonic" worldview and has sought to help people and organizations achieve their best. He enjoys sharing life with his wife Karin and their five inventive children.

Made in the USA
Coppell, TX
02 June 2021

56772587R00121